# REVOLUTIONARY
# SEX

# REVOLUTIONARY
## SEX
How the good news of
Jesus changes everything

## William Taylor

**10 Publishing**
a division of **10** of those.com

British Library Cataloguing in Publication Data
A record for this book is available from the British Library

This book is in no way authorized, sponsored, or endorsed by The LEGO Company.

ISBN: 978-1-910587-40-9

Designed and typeset by Pete Barnsley (Creative Hoot)

Printed and bound by CPI Group (UK) Ltd, Croydon, CR0 4YY

10Publishing, a division of 10ofthose.com
Unit C, Tomlinson Road, Leyland, Lancashire, PR25 2DY, England

Email: info@10ofthose.com
Website: www.10ofthose.com

# CONTENTS

# THE CALL TO REVOLUTION

There can be no doubt that we – living at the start of the twenty-first century in the West – find ourselves in the aftermath of a social revolution. Some have identified the roots of that revolution in the change of our culture's attitudes to sex, which were radically altered with the advent of the contraceptive pill in the early 1960s. Joan Bakewell, who was at the forefront of the battle to change our culture, recently spoke of the mood in the 1960s: 'The liberal mood back in the sixties was that sex was pleasurable and wholesome ... The pill allowed women to make choices for themselves. Of course that meant the risk of making the wrong choice. But we all hoped girls would grow to handle the new freedoms wisely.'[1]

In reality, the roots of the social revolution are to be found much further back and long before the advent of the pill. Recently I had the opportunity to listen to Dr Mike Ovey, the Principal of Oak Hill Theological College, who was discussing the philosophers Hegel, Stirner and Kant. As Mike explains:

*Hegel, writing in the nineteenth century, effectively if unintentionally destabilised the idea of the individual through his stress on continuous progress in which the individual, the state and the world seek to realise themselves. His follower Max Stirner took this a stage further when he said that each individual invents or creates himself over time: we make ourselves. Earlier Kant had argued in his essay on Enlightenment, written in the eighteenth century in 1784, that we should break free from our age of innocence and grow up to maturity, with mature people being those who have become free to think for themselves and who work out their identity for themselves rather than being subject to what their masters have told them to think.[2]*

This suggests that the social and cultural revolution of the twentieth century drew on the key ideas of the Enlightenment and of Hegel, and of others like him. Ideas drove the revolution, as they always do.

Consider what Germaine Greer, author of the groundbreaking book *The female Eunuch*, had to say in 1986: 'Human beings have an inalienable right to invent themselves.'[3] This is classic Stirner–Hegel thinking. Or consider the title of Zygmunt Bauman's book on sex and relationships in the modern age, *Liquid Love*. Bauman's analysis of our Western culture is that we have become 'plastic people' for whom the contours of our identity can be shifted and changed as we wish. In other words, we are reconstructed at different times by our individual choices.[4]

Thus you and I have been brought up in a context where for someone to suggest that this or that form of sexual expression is either better or best, or is inappropriate or invalid, is tantamount to denying the fundamental rights of a human being. Who are you to suggest that my personal sexual preference is wrong? How dare you tell me that your way is better? Indeed to argue that one or another form of sexual expression might be improper has itself become in today's culture akin to immoral. Try it out for yourselves. For example, when asked, 'What are you reading at the moment?', answer, 'Oh, a book on revolutionary sex that teaches us how to enjoy sex as God intended it. It's God's intention that everybody lives his way, rather than go our own way, in this area.' We will pretty quickly find ourselves condemned.

That is why I have given this book the title *Revolutionary Sex*, for I am going to suggest that in the wake of the 1960s a counter-revolution is now required. I shall argue that since God invented sex, God knows best how sex works. It all comes down ultimately to the fact that God is our Creator and we were created purposefully in a particular way. We are *not* plastic or liquid people, who can change ourselves as we see fit. Therefore when we seek to deviate from God's perfect plan for sex, we damage both ourselves and others. There is only one place for safe sex and truly lasting deep and enjoyable sex – in the context of heterosexual and monogamous marriage. Far from God being a killjoy or a spoilsport, he ultimately knows far more about sex than you or I or even any sex therapist does. God understands sex.

I chose this title when I went to see the Hunger Games film *Catching Fire* with Katniss Everdeen. You will remember her three-finger salute. She is not going to be a pawn in the destructive power games of others. Likewise, I am hoping that this book is going to generate in us a proper Christian sense that we are now the revolutionaries who will not conform. We need to argue and act against the folly of the Western world's idea that we can recreate ourselves as plastic people. We need to be clear on the extraordinary damage that the 1960s revolution has done, the cost of which some of us have borne and still feel at the deepest level. I am hoping that this short examination of God's plan for sex will equip us as godly revolutionaries to carry the gospel of Jesus Christ with greater courage and conviction to a confused world.

There is one other important introductory remark for us to be clear on: I assume that every single one of us is flawed in the area of sexual conduct and thought, myself included. I also assume that all of us have failed in this regard, myself included. As such we all have things of which we are ashamed and that we are working through in the context of Christian grace. We need to remember that the Lord Jesus loves to forgive, to redeem and to restore us, so that we can be the kind of people he made us to be.

# REVOLUTIONARY SEX AND CREATION

## GENESIS 1–2

### GENESIS 1:26–31

*26 Then God said, "Let us make man in our image, in our likeness, and let them rule over the fish of the sea and the birds of the air, over the livestock, over all the earth, and over all the creatures that move along the ground."*

*27 So God created man in his own image,*
*in the image of God he created him;*
*male and female he created them.*

*28 God blessed them and said to them, "Be fruitful and increase in number; fill the earth and subdue it. Rule over the fish of the sea and the birds of the air and over every living creature that moves on the ground."*

*29 Then God said, "I give you every seed-bearing plant on the face of the whole earth and every tree that has fruit* with seed in it. They will be yours for food. *30* And to all the beasts of the earth and all the birds of the air and all the creatures that move on the ground – everything that has the breath of life in it – I give every green plant for food." And it was so.

*31* God saw all that he had made, and it was very good. And there was evening, and there was morning – the sixth day.

## GENESIS 2:15–25

*15* The LORD God took the man and put him in the Garden of Eden to work it and take care of it. *16* And the LORD God commanded the man, "You are free to eat from any tree in the garden; *17* but you must not eat from the tree of the knowledge of good and evil, for when you eat of it you will surely die."

*18* The LORD God said, "It is not good for the man to be alone. I will make a helper suitable for him."

*19* Now the LORD God had formed out of the ground all the beasts of the field and all the birds of the air. He brought them to the man to see what he would name them; and whatever the man called each living creature, that was its name. *20* So the man gave names to all the livestock, the birds of the air and all the beasts of the field.

But for Adam no suitable helper was found. *21* So the LORD God caused the man to fall into a deep sleep; and while he was sleeping, he took one of the man's ribs and closed up the place with flesh. *22* Then the LORD God made a woman from the rib he had taken out of the man, and he brought her to the man.

²³ The man said,
"This is now bone of my bones
    and flesh of my flesh;
she shall be called 'woman',
    for she was taken out of man."

²⁴ For this reason a man will leave his father and mother and be united to his wife, and they will become one flesh.

²⁵ The man and his wife were both naked, and they felt no shame.

———————————

Behind all texts on marriage and sexuality in the New Testament lie Genesis 1 and 2. So we must start there – and will continue to return to it – as we discover that God made sex, he understands sex and he knows how sex works best. In contrast the so-called 'liquid love' of our age is nothing less than a lie that is intensely damaging.

## WE WERE CREATED MALE AND FEMALE IN THE IMAGE OF GOD

This truth is stated clearly in Genesis 1:27: 'God created man in his own image, in the image of God he created him; male and female he created them.'

The key point of all of Genesis 1 through to 2:3 is unmissable.

You cannot fail to notice the following in those chapters: God said, God made, and it was so, it was good; God said, God made, it was good, it was so. The point is simple: it is God's creation. He doesn't tell us how he created everything but he tells us that he made everything.

The goal of God's creation is also spelt out in 2:1–3, where on the seventh day God enjoys rest. He made his creation so that he can enjoy the work of his rest in his perfect garden paradise with his people and a perfect relationship with them. Furthermore, the pinnacle of his creation is to be found on day six. Notice how day six is given more attention than anything else. It runs from chapter 1 verse 24 right the way through to verse 30. At the height of the sixth day we find the creation of humankind: 'in the image of God he created him; male and female he created them' (1:27). Five verses give detail to humanity. We are created in the image of God, unlike any other being. Then we are described, along with everything else that God has created, as 'very good' (1:31). These then are the verses that tell us who we are; without them, we will always be lost and confused as we try to understand God's world.

Humankind is made of the same stuff as animals. We share the same biblical day of creation as the animals. It shouldn't surprise us then when biologists tell us that we share 98% of our DNA with a chimpanzee, though we might look at some of our friends and think that possibly it is a little bit more than that!

Nevertheless, we are distinct and different from the animals, and our distinctiveness is spelled out in terms of our unique identity and our specific responsibility.

## Our unique identity

We are created in God's image. Precisely what that means is not unpacked in great detail, though people like to engage in considerable speculation. What is spelled out is that he made us. Look again at verse 27: 'in his own image, in the image of God he created him; male and female ...' Notice the singular 'him' together with the plural 'male and female he created them'. This means that both male and female together make up the image of God. Two separate genders are created with all our differences and together we are created in the image of God. The reason for the two genders is not, as some people like to say, purely biological at this point, as the text and the context show. Some feminist writers suggest that God made us different, male and female, simply to make babies. But whilst that task of procreation is to be found in Genesis 1 and 2, it is not central in verse 27. Verse 27 tells us that we are created male and female to present the image of God. Yes, we have the responsibility of making babies, filling the earth and subduing it (v. 28), but biology alone is not the reason for our two different genders.

Robert Gagnon, who is amongst the leading biblical scholars on sexuality, has this to say: 'God's intent for human sexuality is embedded in the material creation of gendered beings, irrespective of the globe's population.'[1] Here then is the unique identity of human beings: we are created in the image of God as male and female.

## Our specific responsibility

We also find humans have a specific responsibility. Look at

verse 26: 'Let us make man in our image, in our likeness, and let them rule over the fish of the sea and the birds of the air, over the livestock, over all the earth, and over all the creatures that move along the ground.' Verse 28 adds: 'God blessed them and said to them, "Be fruitful and increase in number; fill the earth and subdue it. Rule over the fish of the sea and the birds of the air and over every living creature that moves on the ground."' Together, male and female in the image of God, we are given specific responsibilities to govern and to rule the earth, as well as to fill it.

Now that we've established our human distinctiveness, what does this mean for our understanding of ourselves? It affects both how we define or view ourselves and how we must treat each other with dignity.

## Our human definition

We need to remind ourselves that these verses are to be found right at the start of the Bible and are designed to show us eternal, unalterable truths. Their lasting authority is highlighted by the fact that Jesus quotes from them (see Mt. 19:5) and states that they are the very words of God. Here is unchanging truth – not simply a culturally conditioned truth for a short period of time, but the foundational truth, at the beginning of the Bible, that God made us male and female. Therefore we are not to see ourselves as liquid self-inventing individuals, nor do we have an inalienable right to invent ourselves with lifestyle choices and human identities. Instead we were made by a Creator who created us male and female, and so we find our true identity –

who we really are – in relation to the God who made us. Moreover, as we saw from Genesis 2:1–3, we are created by God for the purpose of enjoying his eternal rest in relationship with him and in relationship with each other under his loving rule. His eternal rest is what the rest of the Bible describes as 'heaven' or God's New Creation. God made us, then, for an external existence under his perfect rule and in fellowship with him and his people.

So we ought not to find our human identity primarily in our sexuality. I remember boarding a plane in November 2012 and, when I went to my seat, the person sitting next to me, a middle-aged woman, held out her hand and announced, 'Hi, I'm Jean. I'm gay.' I didn't reply, 'Hi, I'm William and I'm heterosexual' because we were never intended to identify ourselves like this, by our sexuality. Rather, we are creatures of the living God, who has made us with the purpose of enjoying eternity in rest with him. Perhaps I should have said, 'Hi, I'm William. I'm a Christian.'

Furthermore, we are either male or female. God didn't make us male and male in his image, or female and female in his image, or a combination of male and female in one being. He made two distinct genders and his image is displayed in the two different genders being brought together, as we shall see, in marriage, and not by a blurring of the genders.

Interestingly, even Germaine Greer recognises the distinctiveness of the two genders in her recent book, *The Whole Woman*. This begins with a chapter entitled 'Recantation' in which she says, 'Women's liberation did not see the female potential in terms of the male's actual; the visionary feminists of the late sixties and early seventies knew that women could never find freedom by agreeing to live the lives of unfree men.'[2]

Greer herself is stating that she never intended women's identities to be blurred into an androgynous or mixed being. We are male, or female. Of course there are occasions when, as a result of the damage to our broken world from the Fall, we do discover certain gender anomalies. But this gender anomaly is purely that: an anomaly. God's intention in creation was never for a blurring of genders or a mixing of genders: He made us male and female.

## Our human dignity

It won't surprise you to know that the human rights movement of Western Europe finds its original basis in Genesis 1:26–28. Without these verses and the Judeo-Christian faith there would be no human rights movement in the Western world because it is these verses that tell us that all humans are supremely dignified. We were created in the image of God. The reason we can have human rights is not simply because we claim, 'I am an individual.' Rather, our rights come from the fact that we are each created in the image of God as unique and privileged creatures of his creation.

Once in a while a story appears in the news of a person who purchases a picture for, say, £50 and later discovers that its true value exceeds £1 million because it was painted by a famous artist. It may be that you have never realised quite how valuable you are. Perhaps next time you look in the mirror you might remind yourself, 'I am supremely dignified. I am of immense value. I am precious.' This is not because of any innate quality within ourselves – because we can play grade 3 violin, or because we've achieved a particular accolade, or because of how we look, or because of which family we were born into. Rather, we should remember, 'I am special because, whoever I am, God made me.'

The same applies to everyone we study or work with. We can look at every individual we ever meet, even the people we find a real pain in the neck, and remember that God made them. They are really special. As a result there should be no racism, no elitism and no sexism. There should be no euthanasia and no termination of life. All humans are special because God made them. Everyone has rights.

Another implication of our human dignity is that we are not free to treat others in a way that goes against what God has declared, such as in his perfect provision for safe sex. One of the lies that has crept into our culture in the last decades is that, providing two or more people are consenting adults, it is alright to engage in any sexual behaviour within the privacy of our own home. No, it isn't. She is a created being, belonging to God. He is one of God's creatures, belonging to God. If we treat anyone in a way that runs roughshod over God's perfect provision for safe sex, then we are not only offending against God but also damaging one of God's creatures. The suggestion that what we do in the privacy of our own home is for us to decide fails to recognise that what we do might impact both God's command and God's purposes for an individual, and indeed any number of additional human relationships.


How then ought we to treat the other sex? For that we turn to Genesis 2:4–25. As we do so, we move from looking at how we are made in the image of God to how our existence fits in with the purposes of God.

## WE WERE CREATED MALE AND FEMALE FOR THE PURPOSE OF GOD

Genesis 2:4 is the start of a new section that runs through to 5:1. (The section divisions of Genesis are marked out by the author's use of the phrase 'These are the generations of', as the ESV translation puts it, used in Gen. 2:4; 5:1 – albeit with slightly different wording; 6:9; 10:1; and so on.) In chapters 2, 3 and 4 then we have a distinct section of Genesis put together by the author. He recalls the purpose of the section in 2:4: 'These are the generations of the heaven and the earth when they were created, in the day that the Lord God made the earth and the heavens' (ESV). In other words, these are the building blocks of our creation. These are the tectonic plates, if you like, on which everything else rests. In chapter 1 the author establishes the eternal truth of the story of creation. Then, having told the creation story from God's perspective, he now retells it with the pinnacle of creation, that is humanity, at the centre of his account.

Having described God's perfect provision in 2:5–14, in verses 15–18 we find God commissioning Adam:

> *The Lord God took the man and put him in the Garden of Eden to work it and take care of it. And the Lord God commanded the man, 'You are free to eat from any tree in the garden; but you must not eat from the tree of the knowledge of good and evil, for when you eat of it you will surely die.' The Lord God said, 'It is not good for the man to be alone. I will make a helper suitable for him.'*

Here is an important question: why did God create woman to

be with man? Genesis 2:18 says it was because 'It is not good for the man to be alone.' For many, many years I used to teach from this verse that God made woman to be with man so that they might not be lonely. This understanding makes for a great wedding sermon! For example, imagine Matt and Caroline are getting married. We can say that God has made Caroline so that Matt isn't isolated and lonely. We then picture Matt and Caroline in their dotage, say in another fifty years' time, sitting by the fireplace and keeping each other company – Matt with his crossword out and Caroline with her book. It is a lovely picture, isn't it? Unfortunately it doesn't really capture what Genesis 2:18 is about for the context of Genesis 2:18 makes it clear that Adam's potential loneliness is not the primary reason for God's creation of Eve.

We need to remember why God made Adam. What was Adam's commission? As verse 15 states, it is 'to work ... and take care of' the Garden of Eden. Therefore the reason for it being 'not good' that Adam was 'alone' is that Adam couldn't fulfil his function of working and keeping this world on his own as the male gender; by himself he wasn't fit for purpose. This is why God created woman as a 'helper' for him (v. 18).

The word 'helper' is explained in the ESV footnote as 'corresponding to'. The idea is of someone who is opposite but complementary. It is important to realise that Adam and Eve are equal. We saw that plainly from 1:27–28. God made the two genders 'in his own image'. His image is presented by male *and* female. This truth prevents either male as a gender or female as a gender assuming supremacy. Together, both male and female, they present the image of God. They are also created male and female of the same stuff, for God made Eve out of Adam's rib. Yet it is clear from verses 18–25 that the two genders are made with different roles and different responsibilities. Adam has the responsibility of leading in the relationship, and Eve has responsibility as an equal but complementary being. (We shall explore this in greater detail in chapter 3 of this book.)

The fact that Eve is both fundamentally different to and of the same stuff as Adam is reflected in verse 23 where, once she appears, Adam says, 'This is now bone of my bones and flesh of my flesh'. The author Derek Kidner says of this verse, 'that it is a joyful "at last"'![3] This encapsulates Adam's sense of delight in finding a complementary helper. Yes, Eve's existence will be good for companionship – we mustn't dismiss the sense of loneliness from verse 18 completely. Yes, her creation is good in terms of sexual complementarity, although that isn't explored fully in chapter 2. But supremely Eve is welcomed as a complementary helper for the purpose of enabling Adam to work and keep the garden as they are brought together to present the image of God to the world.

Now, it is in this context of complementarity that the man and the women, two equal but different beings, are brought together in a sexual relationship. Verse 24 shows us the God-given context for safe sex. First, notice that it is a *public union*: 'a man will leave his father and mother'. There should be an open, public leaving of father and of mother as the man now sets up his own unit apart from his parents. Second, it is a *permanent union*. The man is now to be 'united to his wife' or, as the ESV puts it, 'hold fast to his wife'. The phrase 'hold fast' speaks of a permanent, faithful, legally binding union. The KJV uses the phrase 'a man ... shall cleave unto his wife'. This is like the idea of welding, that is a gluing together in a permanent, faithful, stable, lasting commitment. Third, it is a *physical union*: the two 'will become one flesh'. Robert Gagnon summarises marriage like this, 'monogamous (one partner), exogamous (outside the family), heterosexual (of the opposite sex)'.[4] This is very different from the small boy who, in his RE school exam, wrote, 'Christian marriage is one man and one woman for life. This is called monotony!' It is monogamy.

Let me stress again the place of this text in its context. The context demonstrates that marriage is not just set up by the author to be a culturally limited idea that lasts for a few decades or centuries. When Jesus quotes Genesis 2:24 in Matthew 19:5, he does so understanding it be the Creator's word which stands as foundational truth for all of eternity. This means that, for the whole of the time the earth exists, the foundations of the earth that God has made involve man and woman as equal but complementary beings who are to engage in sexual union in the context of a *publicly recognised parting* from previous family ties; in the context of *permanent, faithful relationship*; and then in *physical consummation*. Thus Genesis 2:24, with the bringing together of male and female into one unit, is a fulfilment of Genesis 1:27 – a presentation of God's 'image' to the world. Christians, then, have a far higher view of sex than the world. First, we realise that the physical act of sex with its intimacy and self-exposure – emotionally, psychologically and physically – is so intimate, so 'gluing', that we cannot move from God's plan without causing significant damage both to ourselves individually and to those around us.

I recognise that to write this in the year 2015 is revolutionary stuff, but for a person to move from one self-exposure to another self-exposure to another self-exposure will, ultimately, cause significant harm both to themselves and to others. Second, we understand sex, within the context of faithful, lifelong and exclusive commitment, to be a small picture of the intimate relationship for which all of us have been created – a relationship of commitment, faithfulness and intimacy with God himself.

## God's purpose for sexual union

How does all this affect our own situations, whether we are married or not? It is very important for married people to grasp that the purpose of our marriages is not a selfish, introverted, self-absorbed isolationism. God's purpose for marriage is to create a productive unit in his service, which, as male and female are brought together in lasting union, presents the image of God to the world. The rest of the Bible explains that this involves being in the service of the Lord Jesus Christ and in the proclamation of his gospel. We sometimes find Christian married couples who are so selfishly introverted that we wonder if they have understood God's purpose for marriage at all...

For those who are thinking of getting married, of course a proper understanding of God's purpose for marriage makes it a contradiction for a Christian to marry a non-Christian. How can we engage purposefully in meaningful service of the Lord together with a partner who isn't actually a Christian? Such a partnership often results in resentment as one partner gives of their time in service of Jesus as Lord whilst the other partner doesn't recognise Jesus as Lord. Not only that but it also stalls and stifles one partner's growth as a Christian when both partners are not committed to Christian growth and service.

### God's pattern for sexual relationships

We have also seen that marriage is between two people of the opposite sex, who are publicly committed, permanently faithful and physically bonded to each other. Let's work through the implications of each of these in turn.

## THE NEED FOR A PUBLIC COMMITMENT

As the husband's primary tie is now to his wife, men, if you are not ready for that, you are not ready for marriage. Furthermore, may I suggest in the area of 'dating' that it is pretty selfish to try to bind a woman to an exclusive agreement of any sort outside of marriage if we are not ready to make a public commitment to her. If we are not yet in a position to leave our previous family unit, it is selfish then to demand an exclusive commitment from a woman. Similarly, if you are a woman and a bloke wants you to be exclusively committed to them but is not prepared to state publicly, 'I'm leaving, I'm committing myself to you', then you would be unwise to consider yourself exclusively committed to them – until such point as they are prepared to leave.

### The need for a permanent, faithful commitment

Furthermore, it is only in the context of a husband 'holding fast' to his wife that sexual engagement can be truly 'safe'. Our culture suggests that you can move from one relationship to another to another, without causing any collateral damage.

But as the fruits of the 1960s cultural revolution are becoming increasingly apparent, it should be clear to us that this is a lie. Listen to the High Court Judge Sir Paul Coleridge, who until recently practised within the family courts: 'The fact is that the single most important factor by far in the successful development of children is a committed, healthy relationship between parents.' By and large, our politicians and judges are too cowardly to state what is blindingly obvious to anyone who takes a careful look at the long-term impact of ignoring our Maker's instructions.

### The appropriate context of a physical relationship

The only place for 'safe sex' is within the context of a publicly committed, permanently secure and exclusive relationship between one man and one woman in the lifelong bond of heterosexual marriage. When taking weddings I like to include in the preamble to the service the phrase 'God created marriage for safe physical pleasure', by which I mean safe sex. If only our politicians, social workers and medics were less concerned to protect their electoral majorities and jobs, they would be prepared to speak plainly against the lie that simply slapping on a condom makes sex somehow 'safe'. It doesn't! Indeed, were we to follow carefully God's perfect and good plan for safe sex, we would not only witness a radical decline in sexually transmitted disease but also a significant reduction in the numerous problems, both psychological and social, that have flowed from the sexual revolution.

## SO BE REVOLUTIONARIES AGAINST THE WORLD'S NAIVETÉ

I want to make a couple of observations in conclusion to this chapter. In my introduction I began with a number of comments from various philosophers. Kant suggests that Enlightenment is achieved as we grow up to maturity, escaping the age of innocence. This is precisely the nature of the third temptation in Genesis 3. The serpent said to Eve: 'God knows that when you eat of it [the tree of the knowledge of good and evil] your eyes will be opened, and you will be like God, knowing good and evil' (v. 5). The invitation is effectively, 'Go on and be enlightened. Break free. Don't listen to what God says to you. Grow up. Reach maturity.' This suggestion that we can somehow reach maturity as we break free from God's conscious order is a lie – and for Eve, Adam and all of humanity, the consequences have been disastrous. We read in Genesis 3:16 that the result of our rejection of God's good plan for sex and marriage is a marring of relationships between male and female. Whilst it is important that we learn to think, it could also be argued that the Enlightenment fell for one of the oldest lies in the book! As Os Guinness puts it, 'order without freedom may be a mandate, but freedom without order is a mirage'.[5]

Likewise, Joan Bakewell believed, 'The pill allowed women to make choices for themselves. Of course that meant the risk of making the wrong choice. But we all hoped girls would grow to handle the new freedoms wisely.' Now look again at chapter 3: '"You will not surely die," the serpent said to the woman' (v. 4). In other words, the serpent denied that there would be any consequences to Eve eating the forbidden fruit. Once more the invitation is, 'Go on, live a little.' Yet immediately she has done so, along with Adam, they pay the price, culminating in their banishment from the Garden of Eden and the certainty of death to come. Similarly, the protagonists of the sixties revolution trusted girls to make wise choices, with no mention of any consequences. How naive the sixties revolution was, buying the idea of a culture of liquid love and of plastic people whose contours can be shifted without considering the consequences that would be reaped.

From this we see that the cultural revolution of the sixties, and indeed the century that preceded it, was really part of the oldest revolution in the book – a revolution that began in Genesis 3 as men and women effectively said to our Creator, 'We can decide how we are going to live by ourselves, thank you very much. There will be no consequences. We are going to grow up.' No doubt all of us have frequently heard expressions such as, 'Go on, live a little. Experiment.' Either we are urged to pay no regard to God's instructions or their reality is questioned, much as it was by the serpent as he said, 'Did God really say, "You must not eat from any tree in the garden?"' (v. 1). My hope is that we, as a generation, will engage in godly revolution. We need the courage to point out the folly of our culture, with its idea that we can live as liquid people and not damage each other. And, as we engage in this revolution, we need to point people to the truth of Jesus.

For the truth of Jesus' gospel, with its power to cleanse and transform, provides both a radical alternative to the destructive philosophies of the 1960s and simultaneously unleashes God's power for transforming change. In Ephesians 5:31–32, Paul tells us that Genesis 2:24 is 'a profound mystery' and it actually refers to Christ and the church. There is a man, the Lord Jesus, who lived perfectly in the image of God. There is a man, the Lord Jesus, who has shown himself to be publicly committed to us through his death on the cross. There is a man, the Lord Jesus, who is permanently committed to us and is concerned for an intimate union with us for which we were made. Through his death on the cross, he has the power to wash us clean, to redeem you and me from the mistakes we have made and our failures, and to release us to start to live lives as he made us to live them. That is in purposeful service of him as we present the image of God to a watching world.

# REVOLUTIONARY SEX AND THE GOSPEL

## 1 CORINTHIANS 6:9-20

*9 Do you not know that the wicked will not inherit the kingdom of God? Do not be deceived: Neither the sexually immoral nor idolaters nor adulterers nor male prostitutes nor homosexual offenders 10 nor thieves nor the greedy nor drunkards nor slanderers nor swindlers will inherit the kingdom of God. 11 And that is what some of you were. But you were washed, you were sanctified, you were justified in the name of the Lord Jesus Christ and by the Spirit of our God.*

*12 "Everything is permissible for me"– but not everything is beneficial. "Everything is permissible for me"– but I will not be mastered by anything. 13 "Food for the stomach and the stomach for food"– but God will destroy them both. The body is not meant for sexual immorality, but for the Lord, and the Lord for the body. 14 By his power God raised the Lord from the dead, and he will raise us also. 15 Do you not know that your bodies are members of Christ himself? Shall I then take the members of Christ and unite them with a prostitute? Never!* <sup>16</sup> *Do you not know that he who unites himself with a prostitute is one with her in body? For it is said, "The two will become one flesh."* <sup>17</sup> *But he who unites himself with the Lord is one with him in spirit.*

<sup>18</sup> *Flee from sexual immorality. All other sins a man commits are outside his body, but he who sins sexually sins against his own body.* <sup>19</sup> *Do you not know that your body is a temple of the Holy Spirit, who is in you, whom you have received from God?* <sup>20</sup> *You are not your own; you were bought at a price. Therefore honour God with your body.*

---

## SEX MATTERS

In 1 Corinthians 6:9–20 sexual immorality is mentioned on a number of occasions. For example in verse 9: 'Neither the sexually immoral nor idolaters nor adulterers', and so forth, 'will inherit the kingdom of God' (v. 10). Verse 13 says, 'The body is not meant for sexual immorality, but for the Lord'. Verse 18 urges, 'Flee from sexual immorality.' The Greek word for sexual immorality is *pornea*, from which we get our word 'pornography'. In the New Testament it refers to any form of sexual stimulation outside of a lifelong relationship between two people of the opposite sex who have publicly committed to one another in marriage. This includes sexual stimulation within a relationship of dating or of going out. Sexual immorality includes any form of stimulation, whether verbal (with a flirtatious comment), visual (with a deliberate attempt to arouse another), physical (by the sexual arousal of any one individual to whom you are not married), or virtual.

The last chapter established that sex is a good thing. No one who is remotely biblically literate can rightly accuse God or the Christian faith of being anti-sex or suggest that God thinks sex is ungodly or unclean. Why? As we have seen, because God invented sex. God knows more about sex than we do. That means that God knows about dangerous sex and about safe sex, and God knows how our culture could cure all its problems associated with sex.

We would be wrong, though, to imagine that our twenty-first-century culture is uniquely promiscuous. Corinth was a first-century seaport in the Roman Empire and its writers coined a new verb, 'to Corinthianise', which meant to school in absolute promiscuity. Even what was going on in the church shocks us. We find somebody rebuked for visiting a prostitute (6:15), probably of a fertility cult, and earlier in his letter Paul rebukes somebody in the congregation for sleeping with his own stepmother (5:1). The same licentiousness applies to ancient Middle-Eastern culture and the Greek or Roman culture into which most of the Bible was written. They knew none of the sexual restraints of our age. What you did with your slave girl or slave boy, at pretty much whatever age, was your business. What went on in the gladiatorial arena to amuse the masses makes our public viewing positively prudish. It was normal to visit the cult prostitute in the fertility religions in order to ensure

27

the annual productivity of one's flock, field or herd. People did this as a matter of course. So, whilst it is true in our Western culture that there has been a significant shift in sexual norms over the last fifty years, there is nothing unique about us today. Actually we could well find our society eroding a whole lot further, in the decades to come, as we make the transition to a pagan, secularist culture.

## IDEAS MATTER

We've also seen, from the introduction to this book, that big ideas have real impact when it comes to everyday behaviour. Ideas matter. In the last chapter the big idea was the idea of creation. We were made by God; we are not plastic people and we do not have an inalienable right to invent ourselves – if we think we do, we will end up coming unstuck. In this chapter the big idea that is set to drive our thinking is the biblical idea of redemption. This is the one core truth I want us to grasp: that if we belong to the Lord Jesus, we have been redeemed. For those of us who are looking into the Christian faith, I want us to see why it is that Christians consider our ideas concerning sex to be the best – because sex as God intended it is the best sex. I also want us to see that it is only as we begin to see ourselves as somebody who has been created by God and then has been redeemed by God that we will really understand, and practise, sex in God's world as God intended.

## OUR MINDS MATTER

I guess there are two big surprises in 1 Corinthians so far. The first is that the Apostle Paul has a far higher view of sex than our modern, twenty-first-century Western world does. I wonder if that surprises you? Paul thinks sex is much more special than the glossy magazines do. He thinks sex really matters and he thinks sex is good. Paul is in favour of sex.

The second big surprise is that, once again, Paul wants to address our minds, because it is ideas that matter. We can see that from his continual refrain in 1 Corinthians 6: 'Do you not know' (v. 9), 'Do you not know' (v. 15), 'Do you not know' (v. 16), 'Do you not know' (v. 19). We can't miss it! Depending on our view of Paul, we might expect from him a long list of dos and don'ts, such as, 'You shouldn't touch her knee', or, 'Don't look at this'. Or we might expect a finger-wagging or a ticking off, with a reprimand such as 'You naughty girl', or, 'You naughty boy'. Or we might expect a long list of the dangers of sex. Instead Paul, who is far more in favour of sex than we are, speaks to our mind as he wants to remind us of what we should know if we belong to Jesus. If we don't yet belong to Jesus, I think we are going to find his teaching riveting because, if we accept it, it will change our understanding and practice of sex forever.

## OUR BODIES MATTER

To return to our big point, I am eager for us to grasp that our bodies matter. Our bodies are precious. Whatever the glossy magazines tell us about our bodies, or what we have been taught to think by our culture about our bodies, as far as God is concerned our bodies matter because physical matter matters. He sees us physically as special. Paul presents us with three aspects of our redemption which explain why it matters what we do with our bodies.

## Our body matters *because* there has been a costly reclamation

Here we need to understand what has happened to the Christian in the past. In verses 9–10 Paul says, 'Do you not know that the wicked will not inherit the kingdom of God? Do not be deceived: Neither the sexually immoral nor idolaters nor adulterers nor male prostitutes nor homosexual offenders nor thieves nor the greedy nor drunkards nor slanderers nor swindlers will inherit the kingdom of God.' Now read how Paul continues, 'And that is what some of you *were*. But you *were* washed, you *were* sanctified, you *were* justified in the name of the Lord Jesus Christ and by the Spirit of our God' (my italics). The Apostle Paul wants us to look back at what Jesus achieved for us at the cross: he washed us, he sanctified us, he justified us.

## JESUS WASHED US

Since sex is such an intimate thing – it was designed to be by God – and because sex involves an exposure of oneself to somebody else at the deepest possible level, making oneself exposed and vulnerable to them, so sexual sin can leave a person feeling unclean, dirty and used. Yet Paul says that the Christian person who has trusted Jesus has been washed clean because Jesus died on the cross. There Jesus carried God's judgement of our sin, and his sacrificial death, which paid for all of God's judgement and disapproval of anything any of us have done wrong, cleanses absolutely.

## JESUS SANCTIFIED US

Sexual sin can also leave us wondering if we can ever be wanted by God. Would he ever want us given that we have treated somebody else that way and been treated that way ourselves? Paul says to the person who has turned to Jesus, we have been sanctified. To sanctify is a technical term. It literally means, 'set apart for his holy use'. Have you ever been into one of those houses where they have a particular item of cutlery that can only be used for one thing? Woe betide you if you use it for something else! Never take the sugar spoon, stir your coffee with it and then stick it back in the sugar pot. That spoon could be described as sanctified, set apart for special use. As we trust in Jesus Christ and his death on our behalf at the cross, not only does he wash us but also he sets us apart for his special use. No matter what has happened to our body in the past, and what we have done to someone else's body in the past, the grace of the Christian gospel is such that we have been washed and we have been set apart by God as a holy vessel for his use.

## JESUS JUSTIFIED US

Given that God has such a high view of sex, as we consider our own sexual sin we can end up wondering whether God could ever forgive us. Indeed, even in my consideration of writing this, I have been reminded of my own sexual sin over the years. Yet in verse 11 we see that we were justified. The meaning of 'to justify' is to declare right before God. So Paul is actually announcing now God's verdict over us on the last day of judgement. As we trust in Jesus because of Jesus' perfect life and judgement-bearing death, our sin has been paid for and Jesus' perfection has been credited to us, and so God now sees us, literally, as perfect as we trust in Jesus.

So then here is Paul's first line of argument for us: do you not know that you have been washed and sanctified and justified by the Lord Jesus, through the work of God the Holy Spirit applying the achievement of Jesus' sin-bearing death to your life? There has been a costly reclamation.

My father-in-law is into art restoration, and has been for decades. He loves music too. Many years ago he came to a junk shop in Brighton and saw an old piano that had been used on a funfair for ten years or so. It had been painted white and had pictures of prancing ponies painted around the outside. But there seemed to be something special about it and so he bought it for a knocked-down price, took it home and restored it to its perfect former glory. It stands in his front room today – a Steinway piano. The Christian person who trusts in Jesus has been reclaimed by Jesus! No matter what happened to you in the past, if you now belong to Jesus, you have been washed, sanctified and justified. God sees you as pure. God sees you as his own. God sees you as perfect.

This is hugely helpful to remember, isn't it? I've mentioned previously that the context of this book is one of grace. We are all sexual failures. There need be no finger-wagging here. You cannot write on a subject like this without being reminded of your own personal failure. Some of us may not have personally been exposed to some of the sexual sin that others have, but all of us will have thought things, seen things, imagined things, done things and had things done to us, in one way or another, of which we are deeply ashamed. Here is the glorious truth: there has been a costly reclamation. We have been bought at a price through the death of Jesus on the cross. We've been washed and set apart, and God now sees us as perfect. So to the person who says, 'God could never accept me because of my sexual failure in the past', God says, 'I sent my son to die for you. You matter to me. Your body matters to me. You are mine.'

## Our body matters *because* there will be a future physical resurrection

The next reason why we should seek sexual purity is that our physical body matters because there will be a future physical resurrection. Verses 12–13 show where the Corinthians had gone wrong in their thinking: '"Everything is permissible for me" – but not everything is beneficial. "Everything is permissible for me" – but I will not be mastered by anything. "Food for the stomach and the stomach for food" – but God will destroy them both.' It is important to realise that the bits in inverted commas are what the Corinthians were saying to Paul – Paul was probably quoting from a letter of theirs to him. The Corinthians were arguing that everything was permissible or lawful for them. The argument probably went like this: 'Since everything will be destroyed one day, both food and the stomach that consumes the food, so it doesn't matter how much food, alcohol or anything else I consume.' The big issue lying behind Paul's letter to the Corinthians was that the Corinthians had got into their heads that there was no physical future, therefore they thought all that matters now is the spiritual. Their logic went like this: 'Since there is no future physical resurrection, then what we do physically today ceases really to matter; the physical is now irrelevant if there is no physical future. Our bodies don't matter because matter doesn't matter.' It's the philosophy of 'eat, drink and be merry, for tomorrow we die', which is clearly what they were doing. We see the same idea with Mr Creosote in the Monty Python film *The Meaning of Life*, who gorges himself until, having been persuaded to eat one final after-dinner mint, he explodes.

Paul has already hinted, in verses 12–13, at the error of the Corinthians' way of thinking: 'not everything is beneficial' and nothing should master us. But in the next verse we see the truth that Paul is wanting to drum home to us: God has a future purpose for matter and for our physical bodies. As verse 14 says, 'By his power God raised the Lord from the dead and he will raise us also.' God raised the Lord physically and he will also raise us up by his power to a physical future. Therefore matter matters, and that impacts how we treat our body. If we think that really our body is just like the skin of a snake to be sloughed off, to be shed, then it doesn't really matter what we do to our body, because there is no future for it physically. But if there is a future for the physical, our treatment of our body actually does matter to God. We must realise this. The physical matters to God. Matter matters. Our body matters. God thinks our body is special. Not only has he reclaimed it, but there is a physical future for it. Yes, our body will be transformed: it will be the same body but it will be radically different. Hopefully I will have more hair again and my knees won't creak and all the other things that are going to get worse and worse will be reversed! Yet there will be real continuity with my earthly physical body.

This means that the way I treat my body and the bodies of others today really matters. The motto 'eat, drink and be merry, for tomorrow we die' will not do for the Christian who believes that there is a physical future. This has clear implications for the way we treat both our own bodies and the bodies of other people. Since our bodies have been reclaimed by God and God has a future for them, so we should seek to please God with our bodies. Paul's point to the Corinthians is this: you are not free to sleep with whoever you like just as and when you feel like it.

## Our body matters *because* God dwells in our body

This final point is immensely important and, if you can grasp this, it will really impact the way you see the physical. From verses 15–20 Paul's argument is that there is a new relationship and a new resident within our body. The image is one of marriage and Paul is taking what we learned in the last chapter in Genesis 2 and Ephesians 5 and is applying it to this issue of sexual immorality. Remember that the purpose of marriage and particularly of sex within marriage is to provide an illustration within marriage of the intimate union with Jesus for which every one of us is created. We were made for a relationship with the Lord Jesus Christ who is publicly committed to us (at the cross), permanently committed to us (by his promise) and intimately committed to us (as he comes to dwell within us and we enjoy a spiritual relationship with him). Yes, sex in marriage is both for procreation and for joy and pleasure, but ultimately it is there to symbolise and to demonstrate the intimate union for which all of us were created: our union with Jesus.

Now look at verse 15: 'Do you not know that your bodies are members of Christ himself?' We are actually joined to Christ if we trust Jesus. As Paul continues, 'Shall I then take the members of Christ and unite them with a prostitute? Never!' What a stupid idea this would be. Since sex was designed for an intimate, permanent, publicly acknowledged relationship with one other being, to engage in sexual immorality with someone to whom we are not intimately, publicly, permanently connected is a complete denial of what sex was made for. To involve my body, which is joined to Christ, in that would be completely wrong. Then in verse 16 Paul adds, 'Do you not know that he who unites himself with a prostitute is one with her in body? For it is said, "The two will become one flesh."' The point of sex, ever since creation, is intimate union. Paul's view of sex is far greater than ours or our culture's, which thinks you can just sleep with one person, then another, then another, then another, then another. Sex is not an act without consequence. Rather the Bible's purpose for sex is that we be joined intimately to a person as a symbol of the joining of Christ with his church. So to engage in sexual immorality, even if it is somebody whom we are dating, and to seek to stimulate them physically is to engage in something that is a fundamental denial of the very purpose of sex. Sex is a bonding union of two people who are permanently, faithfully and publicly committed to each other, as an illustration of Christ's faithful commitment to his church. As Paul suggests, uniting my body in which Jesus dwells, would a temple prostitute be totally offensive to him.

With this in mind, Paul urges us, in verse 18, 'Flee from sexual immorality.' I will discuss later ways in which we might do that. Verse 19, though, reminds us why this is so important: 'Do you not know that your body is a temple of the Holy Spirit, who is in you, whom you have received from God? You are not your own; you were bought at a price. Therefore honour God with your body.' Having been joined to Christ, washed, sanctified and declared to be right with God, Christ himself comes to dwell within us. God himself dwells within our body and that is why our physical actions matter and must be honouring to him. Our body really matters because God lives there.

The image of marriage is vital here for it is as if every single believer is married to Christ. We are one with him. We are intimately connected to him. Do you not know that God the Holy Spirit lives within you? Therefore to take this body within which Jesus dwells by his Holy Spirit and to use it in a way which boasts, dishonours and displeases him not only 'sins against [my] own body' but also involves my body in something totally abhorrent to Jesus.

I'm sure you've seen those badges some people wear on the tube with a little tube sign and the words, 'Baby on board'. I actually saw a bloke wearing one of those the other day. I am sufficiently English not to go up and say, 'Excuse me. Are you a biological miracle?' I felt that would be inappropriate and I valued my life, and anyway we all know that us Londoners simply don't talk to *anyone* on the tube! But it did seem a little strange. Every Christian, though, ought to be metaphorically wearing a badge saying, 'Holy Spirit indwelling'. Please don't actually do this! Don't make this badge! But that is how we ought to think of ourselves.

Let's summarise what we have learned so far. I am married to Christ. Every one of us who belongs to Jesus is married to Christ. We are in intimate union with Christ. Therefore to start to experiment visually, verbally and flirtatiously or physically to seek to stimulate somebody to whom we are not actually married is a fundamental denial of the whole purpose of sex. It is a denial of the fact that God has bought us and reclaimed us at the costly price of his son on the cross. It is a denial of the fact that the physical really, really matters to God and therefore how we treat our body matters. And it is a denial of the fact that we are married to Jesus and that he lives within us.

That is how our thinking needs to change in light of our redemption. Isn't it wonderful? Again, please do not feel this is a finger-wagging exercise. Every one of us will, in one way or another, have failed in this area, but here is an encouragement to start to think and act differently. We can be part of the revolution, the godly revolution, to stand against the folly of our age and to say as Christians that we were made by God. We are not just plastic people. We also have been redeemed by God, so our body matters. God has washed us, set us apart for his special use and declared us right before him. Our physical bodies are of importance to God. Now, miracle of miracles, God lives within us. Therefore don't abuse sex and, by doing so, dishonour your body and abuse someone who belongs to God. That leads us onto how this passage applies to our individual lives. I am going to give you a bit of guidance, but really now it is over to you. We are not to be lazy Christians as we read books such as this or listen to sermons. Nor are our churches to be idle congregations. You have just read what God has to say to you from 1 Corinthians and now it is your job, and the job of Christians together, to be sufficiently robust to talk about it with each other. Think about and take time to discuss with your brothers and sisters in Christ what it will look like for us to live revolutionary lives in this respect. Nevertheless here are three areas of application that I would suggest and they are very simple. In fact they are based on three staccato, short commands that Paul gives.

## 'DO NOT BE DECEIVED'

We see this in verse 9, which we have already looked at: 'Do you not know that the wicked will not inherit the kingdom of God? Do not be deceived: Neither the sexually immoral nor idolaters nor adulterers nor male prostitutes nor homosexual offenders nor thieves nor the greedy nor drunkards nor slanderers nor swindlers will inherit the kingdom of God.' All the wicked and unrighteous behaviours that Paul lists refer to a set and determined path, walking away from the direction of God our Creator and instead saying, 'I am going to treat my body and anybody else's body the way I want. I am going to live in rebellion against God.' They refer to what we might call 'a way of life'. Don't be deceived about them. Such a person will not inherit God's kingdom. This is not referring to the person who has made a desperate mistake or had a horrible week, or even who has had a terrible couple of years but now says to God, 'I am coming home.' We know both that we will continue to struggle with sin while on earth and that, provided we are repentant, God forgives us our weaknesses through the sacrifice of Jesus. Nonetheless, we must be clear that the way of the sexually immoral, thieves, greedy and suchlike will not 'inherit the kingdom of God.' We must not be deceived! As those who have been washed, sanctified and justified and as those who are united to and indwelt by God, we must not walk the way of the wicked. We are committed now to a new way of life!

I have just finished reading Alex Ferguson's biography. I have to say that it is a great book and well worth reading. I am not a supporter of Manchester United particularly, nor am I anti-Manchester United, but it is a good read. When Ferguson bought Wayne Rooney, Wayne moved to United from Everton. Maybe once in a while Ferguson had to remind Rooney, 'You've changed sides! You are not playing in that direction, you are playing in this direction.' That is what Paul is doing here. Don't be deceived, he urges us. And when you are tempted to walk in sexual immorality, remember where it goes – to destruction. It would lead to judgement on the last day, when we would stand before God, unforgiven, unwashed, unsanctified for all eternity as an enemy of God.

Do you really want to head in that direction? No, you don't. So don't be deceived. It is really serious, isn't it? Our culture tends to giggle and so forth about sexual immorality, but it is really serious. It really matters. So get your thinking cap on. Don't buy into the lie of our secularist culture: 'Oh, it doesn't matter. I am just a plastic person. How I use my body is up to me. It is all just going to be sloughed off. I can do this, do that, do the other and it doesn't matter two pence.' You will meet God as your judge. It does matter. Therefore don't be deceived.

## 'FLEE SEXUAL IMMORALITY'

I think this instruction is immensely helpful because so much of the stuff that has been written on this by Christians is about 'How far can I go?' Some writers even present us with a sliding scale as to what is OK and even what body parts we can touch of the person we're dating. It is very much like the game of how close can you get to the waves before you get wet. It is a great game, if you've never played it! Yet when it comes to sexual immorality in Christian circles, so many of those ideas are, quite frankly, unbiblical. So what does Paul say with regards to sexual immorality? Remember sexual immorality is the sexual stimulation of any other person – verbal, visual, virtual or physical – to whom you are not married. Paul is unequivocal in his advice: 'Flee from sexual immorality' (v. 18).

There are only two occasions where I have had to flee for my life. On neither occasion did I think, 'I wonder how close I can get to this!' The first incident was with a bull elephant in Africa and the other occasion was because of a bull in Ireland. I'll tell you about this second one. I was fishing in Ireland. To get where I wanted to go, I went into a field with a notice warning, 'Beware of the bull'. What a load of rubbish, I thought! All farmers put that in their field. So I walked into the field where there was a Friesian bull. I know Friesians are a little bit dodgy, a bit temperamental, but I was sure this one was all right. Once I had headed halfway across the field, with my fishing rod, fishing bags and all the rest of my kit, the bull, which was of some size, looked at me maliciously. It pawed the ground and started hurtling towards me. At no moment, not for one second, did I stop to think, 'I wonder how close I can get to it!' I was running for my life. So much so that I don't know how I got to the other side of the river. I must have virtually waterskied across the river because I was fleeing so fast.

This is the sense in which we are to flee, to run far away from, sexual immorality. We are to remember too that we flee because there has been a costly reclamation: our body matters enough for Jesus Christ to have given his life on the cross for us. Moreover, there will be a future physical resurrection, so our physical bodies matter, and God the Holy Spirit dwells within us. We are not to forget all this. We are to flee sexual immorality.

How might this action of fleeing look in practice? If we are watching a certain type of film and it stimulates us sexually and leads us in the direction of sexual immorality, don't watch it. I used to go to a gym and there was a room down the far end of it where the MTV channel played continuously. Many of the film clips were deliberately sexually evocative. I stopped going to the room. If internet pornography is a problem, which it is for many people, both men and women, make sure you only use your computer, iPhone or whatever else you have in public. We must be wise and not stupid in how we handle these situations and temptations.

Once, when speaking to someone at church on a Sunday night, I had this conversation:

*'Did you have a great holiday?' I asked.*
*'Yes, I had a great holiday,' they replied.*
*'What did you do?'*
*'I went away to the South of France.'*
*'Ah great. What were you doing there?'*
*'Camping.'*
*'Great. With anyone nice?'*
*'With my girlfriend.'*
*'Ah right. So where did you stay?'*
*'We stayed in the tent.'*

Immediately my antenna were out. I was thinking to myself, 'I wonder if this bloke is fleeing from sexual immorality.' Of course he isn't if he has gone on holiday alone with his girlfriend and they are staying in a tent together. Unless he has actually had his hormones chemically removed, he cannot be fleeing sexual immorality.

What about you? How are you going to flee sexual immorality? I know of another individual who is tempted in the area of same gender sexual sin. His route home involved passing a sauna to which members of the gay community frequently went in order to engage in casual sexual encounters. I asked him how he was going to flee sexual immorality. He decided never to take that route home again or only to take it if he was with someone else who would help him not yield to temptation. He fled! At college where halls of residence are frequently mixed-sex, it would be wise to set ourselves certain boundaries as to who we might meet with alone in a room.

And for those who are married, or who will be married shortly, do not suppose that just because you are married this is not going to be an issue. Once every five years or so, in every bloke's life, somebody comes along to whom they might otherwise equally have been married. I think that is true for men and women. I have a personal rule that I will never meet with another woman privately, other than a member of my own family; all other women I will only see publicly. You can do that, including within a working context.

## 'HONOUR GOD WITH YOUR BODY'

Paul's final command comes in verse 20: 'honour God with your body'. But what does it mean to do this? Of course this has to do with how we treat our own and others' bodies physically. We've discussed this a lot so far. But applications go further. It could also apply to the way we dress, whether we are male or female. Perhaps we're tempted to think of our body as our own, not God's, and take the attitude that we will dress it up how we want. However, it could be that the way we dress causes others to face unnecessary temptation. I wonder if you have ever considered how you dress and whether it will help or hinder others?

One of the great losses that has come in the wake of the sexual revolution of the 1960s is the old virtue of modesty! Mention the word 'modesty' and we quickly imagine an image of stiff, laced, starched Victorian England. But modesty need not necessarily be a negative thing for Christian men and women. To think carefully about the way we dress and also whether we might cause others to stumble by how we adorn our body could be a wonderful act of selfless service to others.

The issue at the heart of this chapter has been the redemption that the Lord Jesus has won for each of his people. Paul's point is summarised succinctly in the closing two verses of 1 Corinthians 6: 'You are not your own; you were bought at a price. Therefore honour God with your body' (vv. 19–20).

# REVOLUTIONARY SEX AND SAME-GENDER SEX

## ROMANS 1:18-32

*[18] The wrath of God is being revealed from heaven against all the godlessness and wickedness of men who suppress the truth by their wickedness, [19] since what may be known about God is plain to them, because God has made it plain to them. [20] For since the creation of the world God's invisible qualities – his eternal power and divine nature – have been clearly seen, being understood from what has been made, so that men are without excuse.*

*[21] For although they knew God, they neither glorified him as God nor gave thanks to him, but their thinking became futile and their foolish hearts were darkened. [22] Although they claimed to be wise, they became fools [23] and exchanged the glory of the immortal God for images made to look like mortal man and birds and animals and reptiles.*

*[24] Therefore God gave them over in the sinful desires of their hearts to sexual impurity for the degrading of their*

47

bodies with one another. <sup>25</sup> They exchanged the truth of God for a lie, and worshiped and served created things rather than the Creator – who is forever praised. Amen.

<sup>26</sup> Because of this, God gave them over to shameful lusts. Even their women exchanged natural relations for unnatural ones. <sup>27</sup> In the same way the men also abandoned natural relations with women and were inflamed with lust for one another. Men committed indecent acts with other men, and received in themselves the due penalty for their perversion.

<sup>28</sup> Furthermore, since they did not think it worthwhile to retain the knowledge of God, he gave them over to a depraved mind, to do what ought not to be done. <sup>29</sup> They have become filled with every kind of wickedness, evil, greed and depravity. They are full of envy, murder, strife, deceit and malice. They are gossips, <sup>30</sup> slanderers, God-haters, insolent, arrogant and boastful; they invent ways of doing evil; they disobey their parents; <sup>31</sup> they are senseless, faithless, heartless, ruthless. <sup>32</sup> Although they know God's righteous decree that those who do such things deserve death, they not only continue to do these very things but also approve of those who practise them.

---

Before we look at the issue of same-gender sex, I want to make a couple of introductory remarks. First, I know that a number who read this book will have personal experience of same-gender sexual attraction. I am delighted that you are reading this.

Second, the danger of focusing on this issue is that some might think that Christians consider same-gender sexual sin to be a particularly sinful sin. I want to put that idea to rest immediately and say, 'No, we don't!' Rather we are spending this chapter focusing on same-gender sex because the Bible does address this issue, because our culture has made it such a major issue and because there is such confusion about it in the church. So please be assured that my aim is not to single this issue out as a particular sin or indeed to make you feel singled out.

Third, as I keep emphasising, this book is an open recognition that all of us are failures in the area of sexual sin, with no exceptions. All of us have histories of things we are deeply ashamed of and, recognising this, we are not looking to wag our finger at anybody. Rather this is an exercise in discovering the grace of God, who in his kindness and goodness knows the best way for us to live, both because he made us and because he has redeemed us; he has brought us back to himself to serve him and has a glorious new creation in store for us.

Fourth, temptation is not the same as sin. Just as there are people struggling with heterosexual temptation who have not given into that temptation, so it is possible to experience same-gender sexual attraction but not dwell or act upon it. That is not sin.

## GENDER, SEX AND THE BIBLE

Let's start by putting this chapter in the context of the book so far. I have written the book in a particular order for a reason.

So far we have tackled creation and redemption as the two major ideas that drive what I am calling 'revolutionary sex'.

Just as a reminder, we began with gender, sex and creation, looking at Genesis 1 and 2. In Genesis 1:27 we saw that God made humanity in his image, male and female. So we are not plastic people who can define and then redefine ourselves against the Creator's instructions. God's purpose in creation was to have male and female, the two genders, to represent his image. In Genesis 2:15 and 18 we discovered, in its context, that it is not good for man to be alone because man alone is not fit for purpose to do the work that God has given him – the task of working and keeping the garden, and thereby serving God. Therefore God made woman, literally as a helper-like opposite to him. Man and woman are made of the same stuff, but are significantly different. In Genesis 2:24, having made the two genders as equal but different, God brought them together in the union of marriage. Sex then, in God's creation, is a good gift, designed by God to bond two people of opposite gender in a lifelong, permanent, prioritised relationship. And we saw that this marriage relationship was a representation of the image of God in creation and also points us towards the relationship for which all of us were actually created: that is a relationship with the Lord Jesus Christ, who establishes with all believers a permanent and intimate relationship to which he is publicly and openly committed. Of course in creation sex also has the purpose of procreation, that is of making babies. But, within the text of Genesis 1 and 2 itself, sex has a greater purpose than simply procreation. It is there to bond two people of opposite gender together as a representation of the image of God *so that* the watching world can see, in marriage, the relationship for which we were created: a relationship with Christ.

We also saw that these were lasting truths, so it is worth mentioning that Genesis 1 and 2 aren't simply culturally conditioned. The author himself understands that what he is writing stands for every generation. Jesus too recognises this when he quotes from Genesis in Matthew 19. These truths do not just apply to the period before the Fall but for all of creation's existence. I hope we have begun to see that God's word to us in the book of Genesis makes sense of God's world.

In chapter 2 we looked at sex from the idea of redemption and saw that for the Christian man or woman, whatever our past, there has been a costly reclamation. We have been washed and sanctified, and God now sees us as perfect – as justified. Once we were walking away from God in rebellion against him, but he broke into our life, waking us up to the fact that he is our Creator, and he called us to turn back to him. Once we had done so, he washed us clean through the death of Jesus on the cross. One who is deeply committed to us more than anyone else we will ever find: the Lord Jesus Christ. He sanctified us, setting us apart for his own special purpose. He justified us, seeing us as perfect because of his work within us. Furthermore, there is a physical resurrection waiting for us, where our bodies will be raised and restored and, wonder of wonders, having washed us, God now comes to dwell within us in an intimate relationship. So our body is a temple of the Holy Spirit. Therefore in 1 Corinthians 6 the Apostle Paul is calling Christian men and women to be what we have become.

We are not to be deceived by the world around us; we are different. Therefore, we are to flee sexual immorality and honour God with our bodies. He appealed not just to people who experienced same-gender sexual attraction alone: 'Do not be deceived: Neither the sexually immoral [that is talking about heterosexual immorality] nor idolaters nor adulterers nor male prostitutes nor homosexual offenders nor thieves nor the greedy nor drunkards nor slanderers nor swindlers will inherit the kingdom of God' (1 Cor. 6:9–10). Paul doesn't single out the sexual immorality of same-gender sexual activity. The hallmark of authentic Christian living is that we *all* recognise the rule of God, that we repent (or turn around) from ungodly living, and that we experience the grace of God. The costly reclamation that has happened, the physical resurrection that is to come and an indwelling of the Holy Spirit in the present should govern our physical behaviour.

## Paul's audience

I think it is worth noting too that Paul is not appealing to or expecting all people everywhere to live like this. He anticipates that the non-Christian will live like a non-Christian and he expects the Christian to live like a Christian. So I am not arguing that non-Christian heterosexual couples should conduct themselves in a Christian way. Why should they? They don't recognise God as their Creator and they haven't been redeemed by God, so why should they behave in a Christian way? And I am not arguing that we should seek to enforce the Christian view on homosexual lifestyles onto a pagan culture. Why should we? I believe profoundly that God's way is best and I will argue for it, and I know that our society will unravel with devastating effect for our children if we abandon God's plan for marriage. But if a person doesn't recognise God as their Creator and Jesus Christ as their Redeemer, why should they live God's way? Paul's argument is directed to the Christian.

### The new creation to come

There is one key idea that we haven't yet covered in detail and that we need to consider. As I have stated, all revolutions are driven by ideas, and to the ideas of creation and redemption we must add that of the new creation. The marriage relationship in this world is simply a small picture of the glorious relationship for which we are designed in the next. Whatever marriage may have been in this creation, it will not be as it is now in God's new creation. Jesus, the perfect bridegroom, will return to claim his bride, you and me, that is his church, and our lowly bodies will be transformed. All scars, all flaws, all failures and all disappointments will be removed forever and one day we will be in intimate relationship with our Creator for all eternity. Then all the short-term trials of this fallen world, whatever they may be, together with all our disappointments will be gone, once and for all.

## GENDER, SEX AND SOME SPECIFIC BIBLE TEXTS

Having placed the issue of same-gender sex in its biblical context, we are going to look at specific texts in the New Testament, particularly Romans 1:18–32. As we read, I hope we will see that the Apostle Paul is identifying particular behaviours that flow from general attitudes. The general attitude is that of the rejection of the Creator God. Indeed, this passage is driven by the idea of creation. In verse 20 we see that God's 'eternal power and divine nature' have been clearly seen from the beginning of creation from what he has made. The logic is simple enough: whatever the atheist might suggest, we all know that something cannot come from nothing. Even a small child knows that you can't get something from nothing, which is why they so frequently ask, 'Where did I come from?' But you and I, in our wilful rebellion and disobedience towards God, like to suppress this truth and exchange the truth of the Creator God for a lie. Paul makes this point three times: in verse 23, where they 'exchanged the glory of the immortal God for images made to look like mortal man and birds and animals and reptiles'; in verse 25, where they 'exchanged the truth of God for a lie, and worshipped and served created things rather than the Creator'; and in verse 28, where 'they did not think it worth while to retain the knowledge of God' (or, as the ESV translates it, 'to acknowledge God').

What is more, the result of our deliberate exchange of the truth of God (who has made himself plain to us) for a lie is God's measured judgement. Notice the use of 'therefore' in verse 24: 'Therefore God gave them over'. Likewise, verse 26 reads: '*Because of this*, God gave them over' (my italics), and verse 28 states: '*since* they did not think it worth while to retain the knowledge of God, he gave them over' (my italics again). So then, as a culture chooses to reject God, he deliberately gives it over in active judgement to its sinful desires. As we say to God, 'We are not interested in your creation; we are not interested in your loving rule and your gracious provision; we are just not interested', God deliberately turns his back on us and gives us over to what we want – the resulting social and moral disintegration.

The point here is not that one individual will be given over to this particular area of behaviour, because one individual has rejected God in one particular way. This is important. So it is not that the person who experiences same-sex gender attraction will experience it because they have sinned in a particular way. Paul is making a general point and to personalise this passage like that would be a very big mistake. Rather God gives rebellious humanity over to general patterns of behaviour as humanity rejects his loving rule. As we read Romans 1:18–32 we discover that it aptly describes twenty-first-century Britain. That shouldn't surprise us for God told us that as we give up on him and exchange his truth for a lie of our own making, then we will find that cultural disintegration follows. Not only will sexual immorality abound (Rom. 1:24–27) but so will all the things mentioned in verses 28–32. What once were mere gossip columns will turn into whole gossip magazines; deceit and lying will become widespread; the currency of truth will be devalued; greed and envy will flourish; and pride and arrogance will abound. The word of God makes sense of our world, doesn't it?

Please notice once again from this passage that same-gender sexual practice is not singled out absolutely. This is important. It is dealt with particularly in verses 26 and 27, but it is not singled out uniquely. Rather it comes in a broad range of heterosexual sin, envy, murder, strife, deceit, malice, gossip and so forth. Personally I think it is immensely unhelpful that some in the wider church scene appear to have given up on teaching against heterosexual sin, gossip, envy and greed, but continue to hammer away at same-gender sexual sin. It is fair to make the accusation of someone who singles out same-gender sexual sin in this way that their focus on it smacks of homophobia in the popular sense of the word. It is wrong to soft-pedal teaching that sleeping around is wrong or that long-term non-marital sexual relationships are wrong for a heterosexual couple or that greed is wrong but to continue to denounce people who are in homosexual relationships.

Let's look at verses 25–27 in more detail. The Bible states:

> *They exchanged the truth of God for a lie, and worshipped and served created things rather than the Creator – who is for ever praised. Amen.*

> *Because of this, God gave them over to shameful lusts. Even their women exchanged natural relations for unnatural ones. In the same way, the men also abandoned natural relations with women and were inflamed with lust for one another. Men committed indecent acts with other men, and received in themselves the due penalty for their perversion.*

Here we see the unequivocal condemnation of same-gender sexual practice. This is repeated in 1 Corinthians 6:9, which states that men who practise homosexuality, both as active and passive partners, will not inherit the kingdom of God. In 1 Timothy 1:9–10 we are told that the law is laid down 'for the ungodly and sinners', such as 'for murderers, the sexually immoral, men who practise homosexuality, enslavers, liars, perjurers' (ESV) and so on. In his letter Jude (the brother of James, Jesus' brother) also speaks against those who practise unnatural desires (v. 7).

So it would seem that the New Testament texts are unambiguous in their universal condemnation of homosexuality. As I have already mentioned – and the relevance of which will become clear – it is also vital to understand that Paul's argument is rooted in creation. We saw Paul refer to creation in Romans 1:20. He said that God's 'eternal power and divine nature ... have been clearly seen ... from what has been made'. The Creator is also referred to in verse 23 where Paul speaks of him as 'the immortal God'. We find another reference in verse 25: 'They exchanged the truth of God for a lie, and worshipped and served created things rather than the Creator'. Robert Gagnon[1] and Professor Morna Hooker[2] (who was Lady Margaret's Professor of Divinity in Cambridge) have both argued persuasively that in verses 26–27 the word 'nature' (ESV) and 'natural' refer to what is intended by God in creation.

Some, however, do try to take these texts and read them another way. The most publicly known is Revd Dr Jeffrey John, who is currently Dean of St Alban's, a Church of England cathedral. He has written: 'When Paul argues homosexuality is against nature, he does not only mean that it is against the order of nature itself but also against the person's own nature.'[3] Dr John is suggesting that when Paul says a person exchanges natural relations for unnatural ones, he is talking about what is personally natural (or normal) for them. Thus Dr John assumes that Paul is talking about people who are naturally heterosexual and who choose to engage in homosexual sexual activity. Dr John suggests that this comes as a result of a 'false' understanding on the part of Paul, and 'all earlier and contemporary writers on the subject who assumed that there was no separate category of homosexual people'. Dr John argues that 'neither Paul nor his Jewish antecedents considered [the] case of a homosexually orientated person'. Thus, in Dr John's analysis, Paul does not have in mind the person who finds themselves naturally attracted to the same sex. Dr John reasons that the concept of natural same-sex attraction is something that we have only just begun to understand in the twentieth and twenty-first centuries, and so he argues that Paul believes that 'homosexuals wilfully chose their natural aberration'.

There are a number of problems with Dr John's argument, though. The first is that all the way through Paul's teaching we have seen that he is making his argument from creation and thus he is addressing all created people, whatever their personal inclination. Paul is arguing that homosexual sin is not 'natural' in that it goes against the created order. Genesis 1 and 2 clearly show that God made two genders: male and female. Yes, there may be gender anomalies as a result of the Fall and all its ruinous effects, and yes, there may be misdirected sexual inclinations too, but in creation, before the Fall, there are two genders and homosexual activity is against the order of nature.

That point is underscored by Professor Morna Hooker, who wrote: 'It would appear that Paul was describing the idolatry in which man has fallen and has deliberately chosen the terminology of the creation story.'[4] Furthermore, it is not the case that a first-century Jewish writer would have been unaware of and not have been addressing the idea that people were gay 'by nature'. Paul's whole argument in chapter 1 is directed towards the pagan idolatry of the Gentile world.

Thus heterosexual and homosexual licence in the non-Jewish world is precisely what he is speaking about. And long-term, sustained, sexually active same-gender relationships were well-known in the first-century world.

I was out in Nairobi recently and one day I had breakfast with Dr Mike Ovey, whom I have already mentioned. Mike and I were talking about this issue and he drew my attention to Plato's *Symposium*, which has a whole section talking about why it is that some people appear to be in long-term, sustained same-sex relationships which are natural to them, though this is not quite the language he uses.[5] (Juvenal's *Satire 14* also contains similar references.) It is simply not the case that people weren't aware of what we call same-sex attraction in stable relationships at the time Paul was writing in the first century. Therefore the objection some make that Paul does not have in mind, and thus is not speaking to, those who find themselves by nature to be same-gender attracted does not fit either with the text of Romans 1 or with evidence from his time.

It is interesting that the Bible's condemnation of homosexual practice is acknowledged even by those who oppose its teaching. The Church of England commissioned the Pilling Report to write on this matter. As might have been expected, the report declared that it would not consider the biblical evidence in depth, and then declared that the biblical evidence was unclear. Fortunately, though, on the Pilling Report Working Group there was a clear-headed bishop – Bishop Keith Sinclair, Bishop of Birkenhead – who wrote a dissenting article which makes for really good and helpful reading. Bishop Sinclair said: 'Thus, Walter Wink writes, "Where the Bible mentions homosexual behaviour at all it clearly condemns it. I freely grant that. The issue is precisely whether that biblical judgement is correct." Thus Walter Wink pinpoints the real issue. The question is not that the Bible's teaching is unclear. Rather it is an issue of whether we will recognise the Bible's authority?'[6]

Similarly, Dan O. Via wrote in response to the work of the conservative American scholar Robert Gagnon, who I have just mentioned, 'Professor Gagnon and I are in substantial agreement that the biblical texts that deal specifically with homosexual practice condemn it unconditionally. However, on the question of what the church might or should make of this, we diverge sharply.'[7] In other words, even those who support same-sex relationships can't argue with the biblical texts. Likewise, Diarmaid MacCulloch, Professor of the History of the Church at Oxford University, declared, 'This is an issue of biblical authority. Despite much well-intentioned theological fancy footwork to the contrary, it is difficult to see the Bible is expressing anything else but disapproval of homosexual activity.'[8]

## GENDER, SEX AND SOME COMMON POPULAR OBJECTIONS

### 1. 'What about the fact that Jesus never spoke about same-gender sexual attraction?'

We often hear this objection. But Jesus was a Jew and he was speaking to Jewish audiences. So he did speak a great deal about sex and sexual relationships, and he repeatedly drew on Genesis 1 and 2. It simply wouldn't have occurred to his audience, who as Jews were versed in Genesis 1 and 2, to think of anything other than that heterosexual marriage was the only place for sexual practice.

## 2. 'Surely we have a right to express our sexual desires as we wish. Are we not denying Christians a fundamental human right?'

This is on the same lines as Germaine Greer's assertion that, 'Every individual has an inalienable right to define themselves.' Well, I can see the point if we don't recognise there is a Creator. But once we look at Jesus – the historical Jesus, his glorious life, his physical resurrection from the dead, his ascension and his teaching – and then realise there *is* a Creator, everything changes. For the person who acknowledges Jesus as their Lord and Saviour, repentance and faith is called for, together with a dependence upon his strength to battle with sin. We are not plastic people who can choose how we conduct our lives.

## 3. 'But what about some of those Bible passages which seem to suggest an intimate relationship between two men, such as David and Jonathan?'

Jeffrey John suggests that we might be right to see the centurion of Matthew 8 and his servant as 'a gay couple'.[9] But surely we must take care when we read the Bible that we don't read what we want to find into what is written. There is no doubt that David and Jonathan were the closest of friends. However, to assume that they must therefore have been homosexual lovers is to impose our agenda onto the text. That is especially so since the Jewish scriptures, within which the story of Jonathan and David is set, roundly condemn homosexual sexual sin. Dr

John also seeks to find a homosexual relationship behind the centurion's concern for his servant in Luke 7. He argues: 'The centurion acknowledges that he is not worthy to have Jesus come under his roof. Any Jew encountering such a man with such a servant would almost certainly be assuming they were gay lovers. The centurion's deep concern and especially the statement in Luke's version that "The servant was very dear to him" strengthens the position.'[10]  William Loader (who is Emeritus Professor of New Testament at Murdoch University, Perth, Australia) describes such an interpretation as 'highly speculative'.[11]  Once again we must take care that we don't simply impose our own twenty-first-century agenda onto the text of the Bible. Once we start treating the Bible this way, all we find is a reflection of ourselves. We don't actually hear anything about what God is trying to say to us. It is right that we treat Dr John's interpretations with even greater suspicion when we hear that he himself if one of the foremost champions of gay marriage.

## 4. 'What about the shellfish?'!

People sometimes suggest that the Bible's condemnation of homosexual practice should be treated the same way as we treat the food laws in the book of Leviticus. The argument goes like this: 'The Old Testament Law says we shouldn't eat shellfish. The Old Testament Law condemns homosexual sin. We no longer pay attention to the Old Testament teaching about shellfish. Nor should we apply the Old Testament teaching on homosexuality.' This argument fails to take seriously both the way in which God has revealed himself progressively over time (progressive revelation) and the fulfilment of God's progressive revelation in the coming of Jesus Christ.

God's revelation of himself took place gradually over time and was particularly confined in the Old Testament to the people of Israel. His people, the Jews, were deliberately set apart from other nations by a combination of factors, one of which was the food laws. With the coming of Jesus God's revelation is complete and his particular revelation of himself to the people of Israel is finished. Thus the food laws no longer stand. However, his teaching concerning sexual conduct still stands, as can be seen from the New Testament passages we have already considered.

## GENDER, SEX AND SOME SPECIFIC APPLICATIONS

### The Christian believer's response

Again I want to reiterate to those who experience same-sex attraction that this area of sexual sin is not uniquely sinful. We are all sexual failures in one way or another and it would be wrong for those who face heterosexual temptation to sit in judgement on those who face homosexual temptation.

We've seen that for the Christian there has been a costly reclamation: we have been washed and sanctified, and God the Holy Spirit dwells within us. We can't get more holy than that. We have seen that we have a physical future – our body will be raised back to life. So we are warned to flee sexual immorality, to not be deceived and to honour God with our bodies. This applies to every Christian, whether we face same-gender sexual attraction or temptation to any other sexual sin.

Sometimes, quite understandably, people respond to the Bible's teaching by asking, 'What about the intimacy for which I long?' There are a number of ways in which we could answer that question. The first is to remind ourselves of the unique place that God has provided for sexual intimacy – namely heterosexual marriage. In other words, we need to rehearse all the teaching of chapters 1 and 2. Second, we need to beware making, in our own minds, an idolatry of marriage and of sexual intimacy. Our culture *has* made an idol out of sexual intimacy and suggests that we cannot be truly fulfilled unless we express our sexual desires. The Bible teaches otherwise. Third, we need to remember that the intimacy towards which marriage points is found, ultimately, in a close personal relationship with Jesus Christ. One day, at the close of this age, marriage as we know it today will be gone. A friendship with the Lord Jesus is the only thing that lasts. Finally, we need to recover the joy and blessing of deep personal friendships. This book is not the place to explore the Bible's teaching on the subject – for further reading on the issue I recommend Vaughan Robert's excellent book *True Friendship*.[12]

So that brings us back to the battle we must all face for sexual purity. For those with same-sex attraction who think they have an especially tough task, I'd like to remind us that there are many married men and women who cannot have sex together for one reason or another. We would not think twice about encouraging them to flee sexual immorality. Furthermore, we will all know a significant number of single people who are seeking sexual purity. Again, we would not think twice about encouraging them to flee sexual immorality. So too for those who experience same-sex attraction: we urge you to flee sexual immorality and to seek the help of God who dwells within you, and who wants you to live a life of purity. Fleeing sexual immorality is a vital part of being a Christian, regardless of our sexual orientation or whether we are single or married.

Some who experience same-sex attraction also ask whether they should expect a change in the orientation of their desires. Might it be that those feelings are, under God's hand, replaced by heterosexual attractions? The answer is that they may be or they may not be. There are some physical things in this creation that never get changed before the new creation and so I don't want to give you false hope or false promises. But some people do find they change, and some people go on and live a married life even though they continue to battle with same-sex attraction all the way through their life. I do strongly encourage you to get hold of a copy of *Is God Anti-Gay?*[13], where you will find particular advice on this issue on page 44.

The Christian community needs to ensure that our churches are not homophobic. We should not be frightened of gay people and should never give the impression that we hate those who are same-sex attracted. I hope our churches will be places in which non-Christian gay couples or same-sex attracted couples can happily come and explore the Christian faith. My prayer is that, whilst holding clearly to the Bible's teaching, we remain communities of love, of grace, of acceptance and of ongoing prayer for those who are struggling with sin. Indeed, my personal practice is to pray pretty much every day for a group of four or five individuals who struggle in this area.

## An explanation for non-Christians

Many of us will have friends who, on hearing that we are reading about the Christian view of sex, will say, 'Aren't all Bible-believing Christians anti-gay?' When I hear this accusation, I always seek to answer it with a fair recognition of what we have got wrong. I usually begin by acknowledging that I can see why some people might think that way. Certainly there have been times when a culture that claims to be Christian has behaved in inappropriate ways towards gay people. I recite some of the arguments we have rehearsed in this chapter. For example, some Christians have singled out homosexual sin as particularly sinful. Some Christians have sought to impose Christian practice on non-Christian people in an entirely inappropriate way, and this has often led to the persecution of gay people. I then go onto explain that Bible-believing Christians believe that any sex outside of a marriage relationship between one man and one woman is not only wrong but profoundly damaging, both to the individuals involved and more widely in the circle of relationships surrounding them. I seek to outline some of the things we have discussed about why the Bible's teaching on sex is so good and how God knows best how safe sex works. Finally, I explain that this is in line with what Jesus taught on sex, and I aim to point them towards Jesus and his offer not only of forgiveness but also of a fresh start with his help to live differently.

## Our churches' response

The issue of same-gender sexual attraction is an area where the authority of the Bible is probably most under assault today.

In the 1970s and 1980s the Bible's teaching was under assault in the area of the supernatural. We experienced senior Christian leaders suggesting that Jesus did not rise physically from the dead or that Jesus was not born of a virgin or that the idea of him being God incarnate was a myth. But today this issue of sexual ethics is the battleground.

We need to think carefully about the stance that our churches take. Should we cease to speak up about it? Should we just keep quiet? It is not a new dilemma. You may be surprised to know that one reason why David Jenkins (who was Bishop of Durham back in the 1980s) ceased to teach that Jesus rose physically from the dead was to make the Christian gospel more appealing. He and others wanted to make the gospel more attractive in a scientific age and so they took the position that the gospel message should be reshaped to make it more credible to those who could not believe in the supernatural. In truth it was a little bit more complicated than that, but the drive was essentially to make the gospel easier for people to hear. A similar situation arose in the 1990s with the Alpha course, as those who wrote and ran the course were very unwilling to speak about the wrath of God. I spoke with the course authors in 1999 and they responded, 'Oh, we would never talk openly to a non-Christian about the wrath of God.' Today we face a very similar temptation to remain silent on this issue of sexual ethics.

Peter Jensen, the former Archbishop of Sydney, described this phenomenon to me as 'an overemphasis on evangelism'. We are so keen for our non-Christian friends to become Christian that we actually cut out all parts of the gospel that we think they may not like. But if we do that we fail to introduce people to God, as God. We remove from the Christian gospel the key teaching of repentance. Ultimately this results in people thinking they have become Christians when in reality they have not responded to the True and Living God. The result neither benefits the individual nor brings glory to God.

So should we water down what we believe? No, we continue to teach and commend the teaching of Christ. Should we change what we believe? No, because it is clear in Scripture. Finally, for those of us who are part of congregations within denominations where the hierarchy is moving away from the Bible's teaching on same-gender sexual sin, we need to consider how we respond to the hierarchy as it moves away from the authority of God's word. Where a senior church leader fails to teach credibly what Scripture teaches, then we have to begin to distance ourselves from him.

In London diocese, when the sermons on which this book is based were delivered, there were two junior bishops as well as a senior canon at St Paul's Cathedral who had indicated that they no longer held to what the Bible teaches about same-sex relationships. As a result the St Helen's leadership began to distance St Helen's from the corporate leadership of the diocese. It is not right to pretend that there is unity with Christian leaders who dishonour God by a denial of such a core biblical issue.


As I finish this chapter, I want to emphasise that the key message is the same as that of the last chapter: redemption. There is hope for anybody who turns back to the Lord Jesus Christ. Whatever our past, whatever we think of ourself, whatever we have done with our body and whatever we have had done to our body, the death of Jesus on the cross enables our washing, our setting apart for the use of God and for him to look at us and declare us as perfect because Christ died on the cross for our sin.

# SINGLENESS AND MARRIAGE AND THE REVOLUTION

## 1 CORINTHIANS 7:1-11

*¹ Now for the matters you wrote about: It is good for a man not to marry. ² But since there is so much immorality, each man should have his own wife, and each woman her own husband. ³ The husband should fulfil his marital duty to his wife, and likewise the wife to her husband. ⁴ The wife's body does not belong to her alone but also to her husband. In the same way, the husband's body does not belong to him alone but also to his wife. ⁵ Do not deprive each other except by mutual consent and for a time, so that you may devote yourselves to prayer. Then come together again so that Satan will not tempt you because of your lack of self-control. ⁶ I say this as a concession, not as a command. ⁷ I wish that all men were as I am. But each man has his own gift from God; one has this gift, another has that.*

*⁸ Now to the unmarried and the widows I say: It is good*

for them to stay unmarried, as I am. [9] But if they cannot control themselves, they should marry, for it is better to marry than to burn with passion.

[10] To the married I give this command (not I, but the Lord): A wife must not separate from her husband. [11] But if she does, she must remain unmarried or else be reconciled to her husband. And a husband must not divorce his wife.

---

As you know, my aim in this book has been to encourage us all to be godly revolutionaries. The 1960s and 1970s were a time of real cultural revolution, influenced by several hundred years of philosophy. But the ideas behind the revolution were profoundly flawed and we can see the impact of those ideas in our culture as it unravels today. Have a look at the lifestyle columns in the weekend newspapers with all their advice on broken relationships and you can see evidence of the revolution's failure. It is a busted flush. In contrast, we, as men and women with the word of God, have the Maker's instructions. We have God's word, which makes sense of our world. Therefore we are the people with the big ideas from God that help us to understand the world and live coherent lives within it.

I was anticipating this chapter to be the least revolutionary of the four, but I have been surprised that, the more I have thought about it, the more I have come to the conclusion that it is amongst the most revolutionary of all that we have had to consider, especially for the Christian church. This was confirmed to me by an advertisement on the tube which I saw not long ago, which boldly stated: 'God knew you would see this. He also knew that if you are single you would probably love a like-minded partner. Why not give our award-winning site a try: www.christianconnection.com'.

The underlying assumption of this ad is that unless I have a 'special other' who considers me to be their unique and exclusive 'special other' – even if that 'special other' is one in a long list of 'special others' – then I am in some sense inadequate. The big ideas that have been running through this series have been the Christian doctrines of creation, redemption and new creation. In this final chapter, as we consider the return of Christ, I want all of us to see that we do have, if you like, a special One who is uniquely interested in us. If we are Christian, this is what marriage was designed to point to in the first place. If we belong to Jesus, we have One who is permanently committed to us and from whom we can never be separated. He has prioritised us. He loves us. Moreover, he is intimately committed to us as God the Father, through God the Son, dwells within us by God the Holy Spirit. You can't get more intimate than that. Additionally we have One who is waiting for us at the end of this life and at the end of this creation – and with whom we shall enjoy a consummated relationship for eternity. Nothing will be able to beat it.

We must also remember that the present form of this world is passing away. In fact this idea dominates the Apostle Paul's argument in 1 Corinthians 7:29–31, where we read him declaring, 'the time is short'. As a result he wants all of us, married, single or whoever we happen to be, to live in undivided devotion to the Lord. That is the big idea that will be driving this chapter.

I am well aware, of course, that this immediately makes it possible for some to say to me, 'That is all very well for you. You have been married for over twenty-four years.' So let me say that as I write I am deeply conscious of those for whom this is a difficult topic and for whom singleness is a real struggle. I also am aware that the attitude and behaviour of some family members, of some Christian brothers and sisters and of society as a whole frequently makes the issue of singleness all the more difficult. Therefore I want this chapter to be the start of facilitating conversation between us all on marriage and singleness.

## MARRIAGE

### Marriage is for sex

In 1 Corinthians 7:1–6 Paul is making the argument that married couples should have sex. He is quoting the Corinthians who say, 'It is good for a man not to marry' (v. 1). This is translated more explicitly in the ESV as: 'It is good for a man not to have sexual relations with a woman.' It ties in with what we saw previously about the Corinthian church thinking the physical was somehow sub-spiritual.

That was not a unique idea to Corinth. We find Paul addressing it again in 1 Timothy 4 (see v. 4), and throughout church history there have been periods where the church has looked down on sex as somehow a dirty thing. In the third century one church leader taught that the Holy Spirit leaves the room when a couple are having sex. And between the fifth and seventh centuries sexual intercourse was considered so impure that church leaders were encouraged not to sleep with their wives before taking services of Holy Communion. In the Catholic Church the celibacy of priests is still insisted on. This attitude towards sex is completely unbiblical.

We must be clear that marriage is for sex. Of course, for reasons such as medical or psychological ones, there are some married couples who are unable to have sexual intercourse. Nevertheless the general rule is plain, which is why in verses 3–4 Paul says, 'The husband should fulfil his marital duty to his wife, and likewise the wife to her husband. The wife's body does not belong to her alone but also to her husband. In the same way, the husband's body does not belong to him alone but also to his wife. Do not deprive each other ...' That is not to say, though, that the husband or wife can demand sex whenever he or she wants it, nor that the husband or wife can use the other's body to fulfil whatever sexual fantasy they may have dreamed up. There is such a thing as perverted sex.

### Marriage is for keeps

We see this important principle in verses 10–11: 'To the married I give this command (not I, but the Lord): A wife must not separate from her husband. But if she does, she must remain unmarried or else be reconciled to her husband. And a husband must not divorce his wife.' Yes, there are very rare instances in which a person might marry and then divorce, for example due to sexual infidelity or maybe desertion or abuse. However, the basic teaching is that marriage is for keeps. Somebody told me about the time she was having difficulties with her marriage and spoke to the senior pastor of her church (who was an unmarried man), about it. She told me that he advised her in this way: 'You promised in front of all your closest friends and relatives and more importantly before God. You promised "for better or for worse, for richer, for poorer, in sickness and in health … until death do us part".' So then, I take it that divorce should never be mentioned in the home. Separation should never be considered. The idea should never be entertained.

## Marriage is for devotion

This is immensely important: I want us to understand that marriage is not simply about marriage. For this we need to return to verses 29–31, where Paul is speaking about the time being short. Some suggest that maybe there was a particular period of persecution or famine or war that Paul is referring to. But the language of 'the time is short' (v. 29) and also of 'this world in its present form is passing away' (v. 31) is the language frequently used to speak of the return of the Lord Jesus. So Paul's point in verses 29–31 is that whilst husbands are not to ignore, neglect or undervalue their wives (given verses 1–6), nonetheless, because the return of the Lord Jesus is near, there is an overarching purpose to the marriage relationship. The physical relationship itself is not to be the sole focus. In other words, the couple are not to be introverted or turned in on themselves. They are to be devoted to the Lord and his work.

In verses 30–31 Paul refers to those who mourn, party and shop: 'those who mourn, [should live] as if they did not; those who are happy, as if they were not; those who buy something, as if it were not theirs to keep; those who use the things of the world, as if not engrossed in them.' So those who shop, those who trade, those who go out to celebrate and those who are at funerals, remember that there is a bigger overarching purpose to the whole of your life – the Lord Jesus is returning. We were made for a relationship with him, which will be consummated on the last day, but which has begun already through our redemption. The same principle applies to marriage. Therefore in every sphere of life there is something bigger that should govern what we are doing – Jesus Christ will return, so we should be devoted to him.

Therefore marriage is to be governed by the reality towards which marriage points – a relationship with Christ in his service. This means that alongside the internal dynamic of marriage (the physical relationship and the devotion to one another), there is to be an external purpose to marriage. A couple is not to be so introverted and set in on themselves in their marriage that essentially the marriage is just selfish.

The wedding liturgy that we sometimes use at St Helen's is helpful here:

*God has made marriage for three reasons. He created it for* service, *so that husband and wife may comfort and help each other, serving God faithfully together in need, in plenty, in sorrow and in joy. He created it for* safe physical pleasure, *so that in delight and tenderness they may know each other in love, and through the joy of their bodily union may strengthen the union of their hearts and lives.*

*He created it for* children *so that children may be brought up in secure and stable homes. But there is a greater and more important reason why God created marriage. It was God's intention that a marriage relationship should be a model, be modelled on and should mirror to the watching world the relationship which all of us were created for as we serve God in devoted service.*

## SINGLENESS

I want to reiterate, as we come now to singleness, that I realise the acute pressure that our culture places upon many of us. I am conscious that our culture, some parents and, I am ashamed to say, even some within the Christian world put single people under real pressure. I suspect this is made all the more difficult because whilst many in our culture crave deep relationship, our culture is highly mobile, and therefore we tend to find ourselves less deeply related with one another than in a previous age. This longing for deep relationships, set as it is within a highly fluid society, is then often satisfied by pursuing a series of 'dating' relationships that are monogamous and exclusive, but that follow one after another, after another, after another. Within this context there is real danger of Christians idolising marriage, by thinking that everything we crave in terms of intimacy and so forth is going to be found in marriage. So what does the Bible have to say about singleness?

### Sex is for marriage

I want to underscore this point. As we have already seen,

sex is designed by God. He knows how it works best and has designed it for within a relationship between one man and one woman, where the couple are exclusively, permanently committed to one another for life. The word *pornea* means sexual immorality or fornication and is used of any form of illicit sexual stimulation, which in the Bible is any form of sexual stimulation outside of such a marriage. (See 2 Cor. 12:21; Gal. 5:19; Eph. 5:3; Col. 3:5; 1 Tim. 1:10, Heb. 12:16.)

This point is actually made too in 1 Corinthians 7, where we see just two options: if, as a couple, you are aflame with passion, either stop it and stay single or get married (vv. 8–9). The argument is binary: there is no halfway house. The same point is made also very helpfully in the Song of Songs, a love poem in the Bible. There is a refrain that runs all the way through the Song of Songs, where advice is given to the daughters of Jerusalem. It comes first in 2:7: 'Daughters of Jerusalem, I charge you by the gazelles and by the does of the field: Do not arouse or awaken love until it so desires.' Love is so powerful and sex is so precious that the daughters are urged not to awaken it until it is right to do so. The same refrain is repeated in 3:5 and 8:4. Then in 8:9 those with young sisters declare, 'If she is a wall, we will build towers of silver on her. If she is a door, we will enclose her with panels of cedar.' It seems they are advocating locking up their sister – or daughter – until it is time for marriage! In reality their concern is rightly for their sister's sexual purity, and they will take what steps are necessary to maintain this. Likewise, in 1 Timothy 5:1–2 Paul teaches, 'Treat younger men as brothers, older women as mothers, and younger women as sisters, with absolute purity.' Throughout the Bible the message is that sex is designed for marriage.

The most helpful book I have read on this recently is *Sex, Dating, and Relationships* by Gerald Hiestand and Jay Thomas.[1] I would encourage you to read it, with the one proviso that I will talk about later. In it the authors identify most helpfully the three categories of relationship to be found in the Bible: close family; neighbour; and husband and wife. These are the only relational categories the Bible understands when it comes to sex, dating and relationships. Hiestand and Thomas then make the point that the Bible insists that any person to whom you have not committed yourself in the prioritised, permanent and public bond of marriage should be treated as a sister or brother. Clearly any form of sexual stimulation of another close relative such as a sister or child is strictly prohibited in the Bible. Thus, any couple who are not yet married need to ask themselves, 'Would we be happy to behave in this way with our sister or brother?' A wise father would also only give assent to a relationship with the words, 'Yes, *providing* that you only treat her physically in a way that you would treat your own sister.'

## Singleness is for devotion

If marriage is for sex, for keeps and for devotion, then not only is sex for marriage and marriage alone but also singleness is for devotion to the Lord. The Apostle Paul is profoundly counter-cultural at this point, as is the rest of the Bible, and this I think is the area where we need to be challenged most. The Apostle Paul sees singleness as a gift from God and, just as he wants a married person to use their marriage for devoted service of the

Lord, so he wants the single person to do the same for he sees real opportunities in our singleness.

We see this principle in a number of places. To begin with, in 1 Corinthians 7:7: 'I wish that all men were as I am. But each man has his own gift from God; one has this gift, another has that. Verses 26–28 continue: 'Because of the present crisis, I think that it is good for you to remain as you are. Are you married? Do not seek a divorce. Are you unmarried? Do not look for a wife. But if you do marry, you have not sinned; and if a virgin marries, she has not sinned.' Verse 38 concludes: 'So then, he who marries the virgin does right, but he who does not marry her does even better.' For Paul then there are unique opportunities in singleness and the single person – even the single person who remains single throughout their life – is considered to have been called into a highly honoured position. Therefore God wants you, if you are a single person, to think really long and hard about the opportunities of singleness before you think about and seek marriage.

Paul spells that out for us in verses 25–34, which are right at the heart of the chapter. Here we find Paul outlining two reasons for staying single. The first reason, which we have already looked at, is the urgency of the hour (vv. 29–31). If you can stay single, do stay single because the Lord is returning and there is work to be done. So devote yourself to the Lord. Give yourself to him. The second reason is that Paul wants you to be free from anxiety (v. 32). As Paul talks about marriage in verses 32–35, we see that he has a deep understanding of marriage. He writes,

*An unmarried man is concerned about the Lord's affairs*

*– how he can please the Lord. But a married man is concerned about the affairs of this world – how he can please his wife – and his interests are divided. An unmarried woman or virgin is concerned about the Lord's affairs: Her aim is to be devoted to the Lord in both body and spirit. But a married woman is concerned about the affairs of this world – how she can please her husband. I am saying this for your own good, not to restrict you, but that you may live in a right way in undivided devotion to the Lord.*

The Apostle Paul's point is not that a husband's or wife's demands are necessarily anti-Christian, nor that it is sub-Christian to be concerned with looking after our wife – that would deny the whole of verses 1–6. Rather, he understands that, as a Christian man, I have a duty to my wife, spelt out in the marriage vows. I am to love her as Christ loved the church, and that is going to take time. And I must work on the internal dynamic of the relationship if I am going to be able to serve the external purpose of marriage. That is going to take time. Then there are the family pressures: time spent strengthening the relationship, nappies, parents' evenings, school runs and so forth. Paul therefore wants to persuade us to think really seriously about singleness – to value it, to treasure it, to desire it and also to honour it within our church family, because a single person is able to give themselves in undivided devotion to the Lord.

We need therefore to make clear to our Christian brothers and sisters who remain single that we are really glad that they are able to devote themselves to the Lord Jesus at this phase of their lives – because they have the gift of singleness. We need to take great care not to sound either patronising or as if we don't understand the many pressures and challenges which our single brothers and sisters face. Nonetheless, we need to be clear in our minds that we value the single state. A single person may not feel that they have the gift of singleness, but Paul understands the single person to have the gift of singleness until such point as they get married.

I can say safely, without any fear of contradiction, that without the devoted service of single men and women who are using their singleness to give undivided service to the Lord, the work of God in this country and further afield would be substantially hindered. That is certainly true at St Helen's where within both our staff team and the church family numerous men and women are able to give themselves and their energies in the work of the Lord in ways which simply would not be possible if they were married. Some of the Christians who have had the greatest influence on my life have been single people, enabled by their unmarried state to work tirelessly for the Lord. Mark Ruston, for example, read the Bible with me when I was an eighteen-year-old student and helped establish me in the Christian faith. At the time he was sixty-five and a single man, and I was just one of streams of young men with whom he read the Bible one-to-one in single-minded devotion. If he had been married, he wouldn't have had anything like that time. A couple of years ago a close friend of mine came to stay for a few days. He is single, and vicar of a church. In the course of conversation he mentioned all those he had seen in the last few days. He wasn't name-dropping or in any way showing off, but it made me think, 'If he had been married, there is just no way he could have done that.' He seemed to have been everywhere and seen everybody!

Furthermore, we need to be clear that Paul considers that devotion to the Lord is the way in which a person will find contentment in their singleness. This can sound a very difficult thing to say and we might well think, 'Oh well, it's alright for you, William. You've been married for nearly twenty-five years.' So in the course of preparing the sermon series on which this book is based I rang one of our women's workers who is single. I asked, 'Is it true that devotion to the Lord is the way in which a person will find contentment in their singleness?' She replied, 'Marriage is only a shadow of the relationship Christ has with his bride. I have that relationship.' We need to encourage one another not to waste singleness by looking out for one, and then another, and then another 'special person'. Not only does this diminish our ability to love, it also wastes the opportunities of singleness. Instead we should use our singleness. There is a vital lesson here for church families. We must value those with the gift of singleness. Nor should those who are married get into the patronising and hurtful practice of trying to pair people up as if somehow they are only going to be content if they find the 'right person' and get married. Rather, we must all value the gift of singleness and thank God for it.

## Singleness may or may not be for keeps

Having spelled out what Paul is saying about singleness and devotion, it is time to consider singleness and marriage.

As we come to this, I want to tread carefully. I said earlier that in *Sex, Dating, and Relationships* three categories of relationship are identified: close family; neighbour; and husband and wife. When you think about it, though, that is not quite right, is it? Even in this passage – this is explicitly spelt out in the ESV translation (whereas the NIV uses the term 'virgin') – there is a fourth category: the betrothed. Now the meaning of betrothed in this passage is not the same as the word 'engaged' in our culture. Paul says here that if you are betrothed, you must continue to think about possibly not getting married. For this to make sense, we need to understand that in the first century a person could get betrothed aged three or four when their parents would promise them to another child of a similar age, and then they would remain betrothed for many years before marriage finally took place. I have suggested the betrothal system to our family and it has not met with a lot of approval!

This system of betrothal seems alien to us, but nowhere in the Bible does it say that betrothal is either right or wrong. In fact, in the Bible we are not told anywhere what the 'right way' is for getting from a state of not being married to being married. If God has not told us precisely how we are to go about moving from singleness to marriage, then we are right to conclude that we are free in this area. The alternative is to say that we don't believe the Bible is sufficient. There are just four principles that should govern our thinking.

## 1. Understand marriage

Yes, Paul covets the idea of plenty of people remaining single.

Yet at no point in the argument does he suggest that marriage is somehow for the less spiritually keen. Nor does he suggest at any point that marriage is the answer to all our problems.

Those who get married will have plenty of new problems. There will be pressures within marriage, as we find ourselves pulled in different directions by the different and conflicting demands on our time and energy. Once married, it may well be extra hard to live single-mindedly for the return of the Lord. With this in mind, we need to remind ourselves what marriage is for. Marriage is for service of and devotion to the Lord.

Thus we would be foolish to seek to marry someone who wasn't a Christian and with whom we were not able to engage in service and devotion. In fact it would be disobedient and wrong to do so. We see that from verse 39: 'A woman is bound to her husband as long as he lives. But if her husband dies, she is free to marry anyone she wishes, but he must belong to the Lord.' Of course it is wrong to marry a non-Christian, for marriage is for service and devotion. Instead, if we are to marry, we should marry someone with whom we are able to serve the Lord together. Furthermore, marriage is for keeps. We would be foolish to marry somebody we thought was a completely obnoxious pain in the neck. Finally, marriage is for sex. So it would not be a very sensible idea to marry somebody who you thought, 'Oh dear ...' Anyway, we will leave that to your imagination!

## 2. Value singleness

As we've already seen, singleness is not a second-class state, nor is it a state of limbo, nor is it a state from which to conduct a string of 'practice runs' for marriage. In his book *Liquid Love*, Zygmunt Bauman writes:

> *The kind of knowledge that rises in volume, as the string of love episodes grows longer, is that of 'love' as sharp, short and shocking episodes shot through by an awareness of brittleness and brevity. The kind of skills that are required are those of finishing quickly and starting from the beginning. It is tempting to say that the effect of the acquisition of these skills is bound to be the de-learning of love, a trained incapacity for loving. I have had one short-term monogamous relationship, another short-term monogamous relationship, even if there has been nothing physical, another short-term monogamous relationship and another one. What am I learning? How to fail. I am de-learning love.[2]*

We often come across Christian men and women who are so lacking in contentment in their relationship with the Lord Jesus that they feel they have to have a 'special other' all the time. So they move from one short-term, exclusive relationship to the next, to the next, to the next. As Bauman has perceived, what good does that do either to them or to those they 'experiment' with? I sometimes wonder whether they really value their singleness or the other person's singleness. Singleness presents a unique opportunity to devote oneself to the Lord, to grow in devotion to the Lord and to be of service to the Lord. The time is short. We are to give ourselves in service to the Lord.

### 3. Understand sex

We've seen too that sex is for marriage and marriage alone. That means sex is not for dating. Dating is an inherently unstable relationship. Whatever the bloke or the woman says, it could be finished tomorrow. It may even be finished just by a text. That is why it is 'dating' and not 'engagement' or 'marriage'. As a guy once said, 'Without the ring, it don't mean a thing.' It's cheesy, but it is true! As we've already discussed, if a certain behaviour or action is something we wouldn't do with our sister, we shouldn't be doing it with someone who is not our wife.

That explains Paul's command in verses 9 to 36 that it is better to marry than to be aflame with passion. We need to be clear, however, that Paul is not encouraging us to reason, 'If I find myself tempted generally sexually, then marriage is the solution. I must get a wife at all cost. Pick anyone.' Some have taught it like that. And some have said that since each has his own gift, anyone who feels sexual passion obviously doesn't have a gift for singleness. That cannot be the case given that Paul has just spent all of chapter 6 arguing for self-control. To suggest that marriage is basically God's answer to sexual temptation is to consign a vast number of single people to a hopeless non-answer to their sexual temptation. It also causes real problems because if the only reason we marry a person is for sex, we will have big difficulties in the future when everything in that area goes south.

However, as a couple find themselves attracted to one another and as they grow closer, if after careful consideration they decide that singleness is not right for them, then they should marry. Sex is not for dating but for marriage.

## 4. We are free

As we read the Christian literature on dating and marriage, we find that it is full of tips and suggestions on how to conduct ourselves when dating. As far as I am aware, there is no set biblical way of doing dating. It may be that, as we get to know a whole group of people, we find ourselves increasingly attracted to one other person. The issue of sexual temptation may then become a growing concern. We may say to ourselves, 'This is the person who I do think I could spend the rest of my life with and is someone who I could serve the Lord with.' What we should do next is nowhere described in the Bible. Dating is not forbidden. Betrothal is not commanded. Maybe it will lead to a rose-strewn wedding with champagne. Maybe there will be a simple ceremony with coffee or tea. Maybe it won't end in marriage at all as one or other, or both, will decide that singleness is best. There is no prescribed next step of getting from a situation where we have grown increasingly fond of one another to marriage itself. This means that God considers us to be free in the way we conduct our decision-making, provided of course we remember that sex is not for dating and provided we value singleness.

I love it that the Bible is so unprescriptive at this point. It suggests that, within the parameters of his good law, God loves human diversity. We find this to be the case in many similar relational situations. It means that God has given no 'right way' for us to 'do dating'. Instead he leaves each of us, with our own personality and temperament, to explore the riches of human relationships in our own unique way. There are clear protective and perfect boundaries. There is real freedom.

## THE JOY OF REVOLUTION

We began this book by suggesting that in twenty-first-century Western culture those who seek to follow the Bible's teaching on sex and relationships are now the true revolutionaries. I have tried to show how the Bible's teaching presents God's perfect way for us to conduct our relationships. Marriage, as God intended, is the only place for truly safe sex. My aim has been to show how God's plan for sex and marriage makes sense of one of our most keenly felt desires. God's plan for sex is not only 'safe', it is also really good, and where we abandon it we end up doing immeasurable damage both to ourselves and to our culture.

In that sense, as we find ourselves at the back end of a major cultural revolution, Christians in the post-1960s Western world live in a society that has experienced the damage that flows from rejecting God and his good plan. Many of those who read this book will have personal experience of the pain that comes from having lived in God's world without reference to God's word. The glorious truth of the Christian faith is that there is not only redemption but also restoration available in and through the cross of Jesus. Whatever we have experienced and however we have lived up till now, Jesus loves us and is prepared not only to wash us clean but also to dwell within us and bring us to his new and perfect creation. Whoever we are and whatever we have done or have had done to us, Jesus offers us a fresh start with a new destination and a new power to change the direction of our lives.

This, more than anything else, is what God's invention of marriage is all about. As we set out on a path in relationship with Jesus, we will find ourselves to be the true revolutionaries of a cause worth living for!

# FREQUENTLY ASKED QUESTIONS

**WILLIAM**     **AMY**     **CHARLIE**

This book is based on a sermon series that I preached at St Helen Bishopsgate in January 2014. At the end of the series we invited the congregation to ask any questions that they had. As some of these questions are no doubt similar to those on your mind, we are including them here. By way of explanation, and to help you understand the different names given, the questions were read out by Charlie Skrine, our Associate Rector, before being answered by both myself and Amy Wicks, one of our women's workers.

**We said in the series that we will one day be married to Jesus, individually and corporately. That is a little bit weird! Can you say more about that and what it means for our relationship with Jesus?**

**Amy:** I think Isaiah 62 is a great place to go as there God's relationship with his people is described as a marriage and it is described in really loving terms. It is speaking to the people and, in verses 4–5, it says, 'You shall no more be termed Forsaken, and your land shall no more be termed Desolate, but you shall be called My Delight Is In Her, and your land Married; for the LORD delights in you, and your land shall be married. For as a young man marries a young woman, so shall your sons marry you, and as the bridegroom rejoices over the bride, so shall your God rejoice over you' (ESV). That last sentence is the key bit.

So imagine or try to remember the most devoted, adoring groom's speech at a wedding that you have been to in the last few years, where you have thought, 'This guy is so chuffed. He is totally over the moon about his bride.' That is a flickering, shadowy version of how God feels about his people and that is a true statement about the relationship that we have with God. It is not just trite in a kind of 'God loves you' way. It is actually more true than the devotion a groom has for his bride. And I think as we dwell on that – realising that is the exact relationship we have with God and one which will become perfectly clear in the future, in the new creation, when we are with him – then it helps us to see that all those longings that we have for marriage as single people are right longings to have, but if you hope they will be entirely fulfilled in a human husband on this earth, then you will be disappointed. But if you are convinced that they will be satisfied ultimately in the new creation in that relationship with God, then you will be satisfied.

**William:** That is extremely helpful. Also in Revelation 21 the church is described as being dressed as a 'bride adorned for her husband' (v. 2, ESV) with all pictures being of Christ washing us and preparing us for him. Ephesians 5 states of marriage, 'This is a profound mystery – but I am talking about Christ and the church.' Again Christ nourishes and cherishes his bride, the church. The selfless, permanent, committed love of Jesus for us is in all of those sort of pictures, isn't it?

### William, where does your definition of sexual morality come from? You have defined sexual morality very specifically.

**William:** I have because of *pornea*. *Pornea* is the Greek word for fornication. It is all sexual immorality, all sexual intercourse outside marriage. But because so much else leads up to sex – anything that is sexually stimulating is designed to lead to sex – all of that is also understood to be purely within marriage. So keep the marriage bed pure. 1 Timothy 5:1-2: 'Treat … women as sisters, with absolute purity.' I chose to use Solomon's Song of Songs particularly because of this principle of 'Don't let love out of the box'. Sexual pre-intercourse stimulation is designed to let love out of the box – that is exactly what it is designed for. Within 1 Corinthians 7, if you find yourself aflamed with passion (v. 9), then the time has come either to get married or to say actually, 'No, singleness is for me. I understand marriage and marriage is not for this relationship.' Then do exactly what 1 Corinthians 6 says: 'Flee from sexual immorality' (v. 18). We are not fleeing sexual immorality if we are seeing how far we can go or are going a part of the way but not going the whole way. That is not fleeing sexual immorality. To con yourself that it is, I am afraid, is playing games with God's word.

### *If somebody wants to do further work about what the word means, what sort of homework would you set?*

**Charlie:** I would look at all those passages. So look up sexual immorality and trace its meaning through the Bible. Then look up 1 Timothy 5:2, written to Timothy as a young elder who is meant to be a model to the church: '[Treat] younger women as sisters, with absolute purity.' Look up the verses in the Song of Solomon and see what we are to do. Then look at the way Paul talks about sexual morality in 1 Corinthians 6 in terms of fleeing from it and instead honouring God with your body.

### *Though these questions are not quite on our topic, first, should adultery lead to divorce? Second, if you are a divorced person, is it OK to seek to be married?*

**William:** Adultery does not necessarily lead to divorce, need not necessarily lead to divorce and I know of a number of cases where it has not. So at all cost, if you possibly can, seek to sustain the relationship and put it back together. The gospel will really help you on that. And find help too.

So adultery need not lead to divorce. But the Bible views sex much more highly than we do and the Bible, that is God, understands sex to join a person to another person. Therefore a sustained adulterous relationship outside of marriage obviously effectively smashes the covenant bond.

Christians disagree on whether remarriage is possible and I would encourage you to talk personally to somebody about that rather than tackle it publicly as it needs much longer.

*Someone here comes from a family where the relations between father and mother are unhappy. I guess that will be true of a lot of people here. She has a difficult time accepting Jesus' teaching that marriage is for life. She thinks her parents should divorce. What would you say to someone in that situation?*

**Amy:** Jesus' teaching can be hard to accept, especially when you are watching people struggle in their marriage. However, we also know that Jesus is perfectly wise and that his teaching is good. So we need to trust him, and accept his teaching. I guess when it comes to parents and children, it is very hard for children or even grown-up children to be involved in that situation. The most important thing is to pray for your parents. If they are Christians, then encourage them in their relationship with Jesus. I would also hope that they would get help from their church to work on their marriage and stay together.

**William:** I want to begin by challenging the lie that what we do individually or what we do as a couple – providing it doesn't do anybody else any harm –

is an isolated act and therefore we should look only towards the happiness of any particular couple rather than its corporate impact. We only need to think about that for thirty seconds to realise that is a complete nonsense. The lie has come out of Enlightenment thinking, John Stuart Mill's predominantly, and alleges that we should be free to do whatever we like in the privacy of our own home and as long as it doesn't hurt anybody else. But actually the breakdown of a marriage impacts a whole range of people and we know this. Broken marriage relationships profoundly affect children and wider networks of relationships far beyond anything we realise. The muddle the French have got into with Monsieur Hollande's sexual liaisons is an illustration of this. Some say surely what he does in the privacy of his own home doesn't matter, but his behaviour not only damages the first lady (as can be seen from her reaction) but also undermines the whole foundation of marriage in French culture. Likewise, when Robin Cook had an affair a few years back, he did it in the privacy of his own governmental office and the line was spun that it didn't harm anyone else. But that was patently untrue. This lie of convenience has been bought by our secularist culture. As godly revolutionaries we should challenge it at the very deepest level. When it comes to an individual claiming, 'Oh we would be much happier apart', possibly that may be the case, but it is always easier to see things that might be rather than the damage that is going to be done to the two parties as well as to the wide network of additional relationships that will be impacted. For this reason we should do everything we possibly can to save marriages and help couples work together at staying together.

**Can a gay person (i.e. someone who experiences same-sex attraction) be a preacher if they are repentant and are not practising homosexual acts?**

**William:** Absolutely 100% yes. Yes, of course! And why ever not? Look back at chapter 3. Can a heterosexual person who is single or married and experiences sexual attraction preach? Yes, otherwise there wouldn't be any preachers anywhere!

**What are some helpful ways to care for and love a Christian friend who experiences same-sex attraction?**

**Amy:** Just be a Christian friend to them. That means spending time with them and listening to them. There are all sorts of helpful questions which you can ask so that you can understand exactly what they are struggling with. So ask them, for example, 'What's it like for you? What makes that hard? What do you think would help?' Encourage them in their everyday walk with Jesus because actually that is the thing that is going to help them keep going as a Christian. In lots of ways the answer is the same for how would you help a friend struggling with any kind of sin; be a Christian friend to them. As mentioned previously, Vaughan Roberts has written a great book on friendship, called *True Friendship*, so why not read that if you are not sure how to be a Christian friend. But otherwise it's about spending time with them and doing a good job of listening to, understanding and encouraging them. Be prepared to invest in them.

**William:** I think as people go on in ten, fifteen or twenty years' time, some of us will be married and so forth, and we can involve them in our family. But close Christian friendship is hugely important. We have got to be better friends to them than anybody else, if you see what I mean. That is really, really important. There should be in St Helen's, as I've said before, no sense of judgementalism over somebody who experiences same-sex attraction.

 **Amy:** Can I add one thing? Don't let this be the only issue that defines the friendship. Don't let that be the only topic of conversation because that probably fosters the idea that it's the thing that identifies them – and it is not. It is an aspect of their Christian life. So talk widely about being a Christian but don't be afraid to address that topic either.

***Married couples tend to hang out with other married couples. Single people tend to hang out with other single people. Is that exacerbating our problems with discontentment?***

 **Charlie:** I think the answer is in the question. It is an excellent question, and particularly with people who are same-sex attracted in mind. If married people are only friends with married people, that really is annoying for other people in the group. So if we could all try to have general friendships across all sorts of circumstances and not just invest in the people in the same situation as us, that would be very helpful.

 **William:** But don't feel you have to take on the world. I think if each family in our church had deep relationships with one or two single people, that would just be such a help, whereas shallow relationships with lots of people are not so helpful. So for families to have single friends who are really close to children growing up and so forth is hugely helpful. May I say just how grateful we are to those who have befriended our kids. We will come across, as we go on, a few people who we can embrace into family life. And that is much better than, say, once a year having a special party for all our single friends. That is enough to make them all sick!

### Is remarriage or marriage to a non-Christian really sin or is just unadvisable?

**William:** Well the Old Testament treats it as a sin and you then have to ask does that come through into the New Testament, and yes it is restated there. I Corinthians 7:39–40 states, 'A woman is bound to her husband as long as he lives. But if her husband dies, she is free to marry anyone she wishes, but he must belong to the Lord.' The teaching is very clear that she – and therefore anyone else – is only to marry a Christian person.

### There are lots of questions on singleness. One challenges what William said that it is good to be single. How about the fact that in Genesis it says, 'It is not good for the man to be alone' (2:18)?

**William:** I would like to take us back and think about Genesis 2:18. 'It is not good for the man to be alone' is given in the context of Genesis 2:15 where Adam is given the responsibility of caring for, tending and guarding the garden and serving God in the garden. So the female gender is created because the male gender alone is not adequate for this task. It is in that context, then, that male and female are brought together in marriage. So I don't want to undermine what 2:18 says. For those who do get married, it is really good to know that the two genders are brought together in a specific marriage to present the image of God (see 1:26) to the watching world. But Genesis 2:18 comes before Genesis 2:24, not after, so 2:18 is a point at that stage about gender generally before it then gets honed down in 2:24 into marriage specifically.

**Charlie:** So the fact that the species or the gender can't do the task alone doesn't mean you individually can't.

*The next question is the opposite approach. As 1 Corinthians 7 clearly states that it is better where possible to stay single and not get married at all, why are you therefore not teaching that everyone should stay single if they are able?*

**William:** Well, because of verse 38: 'he who marries his betrothed does well, and he who refrains from marriage will do even better' (ESV). And because of verse 35: 'I am saying this for your own good, not to restrict you'. So Paul is quite deliberately not doing what you have just suggested. He is saying there are great benefits in staying single, but that if you get married, you haven't done a bad thing. In fact, in verse 38, you have done 'well' to marry. So don't push beyond what the Bible says.

I love the Bible. The more you read the Bible, the more brilliant it is. And as you come to individual verses, you think you just could not have put it more brilliantly. And the careful way in which the Apostle doesn't undermine marriage but exalts marriage and holds it up whilst at the same time advocating the benefits of singleness is just brilliant. It is one of the reasons why I believe the Bible is God's word. No human being could have written a book like that.

### *Amy, how can you have a gift for singleness? I guess within that question, what is that gift?*

**Amy:** That is a good question, isn't it? Because there are as many views on that question as there are books on dating and singleness, as far as I can tell. The nature of my job means I have a whole shelf on this subject. Everyone comes up with a different answer. You have the full spectrum of ideas. There are those that say if you want to be married, you clearly don't have the gift of singleness, so it is going to be 'OK'. Then some say that certain people definitely have a particular type of gift, such as some type of temperament, that means you are particularly gifted towards singleness and therefore you are not going to be thinking about marriage all the time. Other books say just bonkers things about singleness and why you might be single.

Paul seems to think that, whether you are single or you are married, you should be devoted to the Lord. So if you are single now, you have the gift of singleness today, and therefore use it for the Lord. And if in a year's time you find yourself married, however you have got from A to B, use it to be devoted to the Lord.

**Charlie:** So the gift of singleness is not a special superpower?

**Amy:** No. I mean I think some people are perhaps more disposed to being able to cope with singleness, but broadly speaking if you are single, you probably think about getting married, don't you sometimes? But the point is to learn contentment today in your circumstances that God has put you in and to use every opportunity that you have to be devoted to the Lord. Don't think that being a women's worker means I have some special gene that means I don't care about marriage or don't want to be married. That's not true. I am a woman. I am thirty–two. I am single. I think about marriage! But you and I have the circumstances we are in today and they are given to us by God, so we should use them for the gospel. And actually we should be really excited about that opportunity because, if you look around the room, there are five hundred of us here. If we think about it, in the world's terms, we are probably among the healthiest, wealthiest, most mobile, well-educated, and well-taught (in terms of the gospel) group of people. You could do anything for the gospel, so don't worry too much that you haven't got a husband or a wife!

**William:** I think this question is a misunderstanding of the gifts, so I would want to encourage you to go and look at Romans 12, 1 Corinthians 12 and I Peter 5, and then ask what is there in any of these gift lists to say that a person should necessarily feel good about exercising their gift. There is nothing in that list. For example, I know plenty of gospel teachers who find speaking publicly difficult – I do not like speaking publicly. You may think I love the sound of my own voice, but I don't.

**What about the single woman's maternal desires? A woman's desires can sometimes be overwhelming. How do you reconcile singleness with wanting a child?**

 **Amy:** It is so hard and I think singleness definitely goes through different seasons. When you are twenty-one, you think, 'I want a boyfriend.' In your late twenties everyone is getting married and that can be a nightmare for single people. Then in your thirties everyone is having babies. And for women there is a time limit on having babies. That is just biology, isn't it? So it is hard because it is a real ache, and you know that it might not happen and you have to grieve it slightly. That is a really hard part of singleness.

But Jesus' words are so precious. Mark 10 is a great place to turn to. Peter says to Jesus, 'We have left everything to follow you!' (v. 28). Jesus accepts that yes they have, but then adds: 'no-one who has left home or brothers or sisters or mother or father or children or fields for me and the gospel will fail to receive a hundred times as much in this present age' (vv. 29–30). And that is true. We are a church and Christian family in a more true sense than you are family with your blood brothers and sisters. That means that as I look out here, I have 500 big or little brothers and sisters. And actually for the families that I get to know well at church, I have some little brothers and sisters that I am Aunty Amy to. As you get to know people really well, that is a really precious thing and means that you can be part of a family, get to know the children and be part of raising and having an influence on them. And you get the massive benefit that you don't have the sleepless nights! In that respect it is a win-win situation.

So that maternal desire is real. It is painful at times. But there are lots of ways to work it out in a church family which is real family.

**Charlie:** I speak as a parent. Culturally there is now a huge suspicion of adults being interested in other people's children and we have to be very careful. So we are very strict about child protection, safeguarding and vetting people for our children's work. But as a parent I am delighted when other adults are interested in my children. Our culture has become bizarre, particularly for men, in terms of suggesting that there must be something wrong with you if you are happy to have a conversation with a six-year-old. But that is a wonderful church family thing, within appropriate safeguards and carefulness.

### *Do you have any tips on how married couples can value singleness more without being patronising to single people?*

**Amy:** The set-up dinner party isn't that much fun. It is a bit of a nightmare, isn't it?! Also, don't let a person's singleness be the only topic of conversation. I had a boss for a while who was a great, great boss. But when I started working for him, he would at the end of every meeting go, 'Who is it? Who is it?' And there wasn't anyone. After about five years it turned to, 'Who is there? There must be someone!' It was totally demoralising. So don't say things like that to single people. And at weddings don't say, 'You'll be next' or 'He's out there somewhere!' If you are a parent, don't write a Christmas letter that says a lot about your sons getting married and has one line about the daughter that says, 'She is still living in London and waiting for Mr Darcy!'

*There are many questions about dating. Different people have different relationships with their brothers and sisters. How do we discern the right way to treat a boyfriend or girlfriend like a brother or sister? Or, if you aren't husband and wife, then what would a dating relationship look like so that it was physically like siblings? Would you commit to each other in an exclusive sense? How should you spend time together and learn about each other's lives? Should you hang out with members of the other gender? In other words, what is different when you are dating someone?*

 **William:** Well, I think I would want to encourage people that I don't think there are rules. So we are now heading into the area that we are essentially free providing we understand marriage, value singleness and understand sex.

Now on the sister and brother thing, I spoke deliberately on sibling sexual activity because it is wrong. But speaking in terms of a proper relationship between brothers and sisters, I haven't in a million years ever contemplated seeking to hug my sister in an inappropriately sexually intimate way or to kiss her like that. It seems to me Paul is saying if you wouldn't do that with your sister, don't do that with someone you are only going out with. A dating relationship may be gone tomorrow. It may be finished, whatever he or she says. It is inherently unstable.

In terms of friendships, I think the idea of having lots of friends – of both genders – is great. Then make sure as you get to know somebody better that you protect those boundaries and don't put yourself in a tempting situation. Flee sexual immorality. Of course you are going to have to get to know somebody better and I love it that people go away on mixed houseparties together. I think it is fantastic that people go away together walking, climbing, skiing, camping and all these sorts of things. That is an ideal place to be getting to know somebody really well and then, whether it is meeting up for coffee or whatever – hopefully it is something a bit more imaginative! – you may then say, 'I would be really interested in getting to know you a bit better.' But if we are clear on marriage and clear on singleness and clear on sex, then we are free to conduct the 'dating' as we wish.

**Amy:** Don't act like there is more commitment than there is. Don't act like a married couple when you are not married because, as the commitment is not there, it could end tomorrow.

In terms of emotional investment, I think guys should understand that if you make too many declarations of your feelings before you are ready to commit, you put the girl in real danger of giving herself to you emotionally before she should have. And then if you decide that you are not going to pursue the relationship, you really ruin her for the next guy. It is a much bigger mess to clear up. So guard your heart. Don't give yourself away emotionally before you should.

**William:** Men, if you are going to be leading in a relationship of marriage, then lead in dating. That doesn't mean splurging out in an insecure way and making promises of commitment which you are just not ready to make. When you are ready, then talk in that sort of way; but before you are ready, don't. I think such false declarations are extremely unhelpful because they go against the command: 'Husbands, love your wives, just as Christ loved the church' (Eph. 5:25). It goes against that essential biblical foundation to a relationship.

# NOTES

### The Call to Revolution

1. Joan Bakewell, writing in the *Radio Times*, June 2010.

2. Dr Mike Ovey was speaking here in a private conversation.

3. Germaine Greer, quoted in *The Times*, 2 February 1986.

4. Zygmunt Bauman, *Liquid Love* (Polity Press, 2003).

### Revolutionary Sex and Creation

1. Dan O. Via and Robert A.J. Gagnon, *Homosexuality and the Bible* (Augsburg Fortress, 2003), p. 58.

2. Germaine Greer, *The Whole Woman* (Doubleday, 1999), p. 2.

3. Derek Kidner, *Genesis* (Tyndale Press, 1967), p. 66.

4. Robert A.J. Gagnon, *The Bible and Homosexual Practice* (Abingdon Press, 2002), p. 62, footnote 51.

5. Os Guinness, *A Free People's Suicide* (IVP, 2012), p. 54.

## Revolutionary Sex and Same-Gender Sex

1.  Robert A.J. Gagnon, *The Bible and Homosexual Practice*, p. 254.

2.  M.D. Hooker, 'Adam in Romans 1' from *New Testament Studies 6* (1960), p. 300.

3.  Jeffrey John, *Permanent, Faithful, Stable* (DLT, 2012), p. 18.

4.  M.D. Hooker, *New Testament Studies* 6, p. 300.

5.  For those wanting to read more about this and from a biblical viewpoint, I suggest two major works: Robert A.J. Gagnon's *The Bible and Homosexual Practice* and William Loader's *The New Testament on Sexuality* (William B. Eerdmans Publishing Company, 2012), The latter is over 550 pages long but has a whole section on Plato's Symposium.

6.  Quoted in Report of the House of Bishops Working Group on Human Sexuality (Church House Publishing, 2013), p. 136, paragraph 467.

7.  Quoted in Report of the House of Bishops Working Group on Human Sexuality, p. 136, paragraph 467.

8.  Quoted in Report of the House of Bishops Working Group on Human Sexuality, p. 136, paragraph 467.

9.  Jeffrey John, *Permanent, Faithful, Stable*, p. 18.

10. Jeffrey John, *Permanent, Faithful, Stable*, pp. 14–15.

11. William Loader, *The New Testament on Sexuality*, p. 337.

12. Vaughan Roberts, *True Friendship* (10Publishing, 2013).

13. Sam Allbery, *Is God Anti-Gay?* (The Good Book Company, 2013).

## Singleness and Marriage and the Revolution

1. Gerald Hiestand and Jay Thomas, *Sex, Dating, and Relationships* (Crossway, 2012).

2. Zygmunt Bauman, *Liquid Love* (Polity Press, 2003).

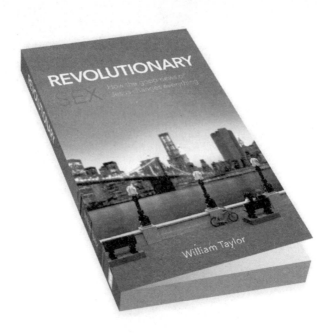